I'll Never Ask Why Again, I'll Just Believe

Jan Dickensheet
with Reta Spears-Stewart

Barnabas Publishing Services

I'll Never Ask Why Again,
I'll Just Believe
© 1998 by Janis Talbert Dickensheet
Cover design and Matrix by Phillip Secca
Edited by Reta Spears-Stewart
First Edition, Published, 1998,
Barnabas Publishing Services,
2150 S. Fairway, Ste. 203
Springfield, Missouri, 65804 U.S.A.
Printed by Color-Graphic, Inc.
Springfield, Missouri, U.S.A.

All rights reserved. No portion of this book may be reproduced in any form or by any means—electronic, mechanical, photocopy, recording, or any other—without the written permission of the author, with the exception of brief excerpts in printed reviews.

Library of Congress Catalog Card Number: 98-072430
ISBN 1-892477-04-1

This book is for you Lord, because you told me this is what you wanted me to do. It is also dedicated to the memory of our son David Alan Dickensheet and his wife Terri, to our older son Steve, his wife Myra and their son Kelby, to my husband George who has been my silent support through the years and to those who follow in a faith walk with a loving God.

Thank You, Lord, for my friend Ruth and her idea of using my artistic abilities to release from my mind to paper these experiences and the insights gained from them.

God bless you all,
Jan Dickensheet

Colors of the Chapters of My Life

In this matrix, I feel the Lord has given me a way to put my life experiences, and the insights gained from them, in an orderly fashion. In the artist part of my mind, colors have helped to congeal the glorious things He has taught me. Perhaps it will help you to apply some of these discernments to your life, too:

Chapter One, Beginnings — Gray, the past, a mixture of light and dark
Chapter Two, Holy Communion — White, the purity of the Holy Spirit
Chapter Three, Living My Prayers — Green, the color of life, breath and growth
Chapter Four, Symbols — Red, God's power — a cardinal...and Dave
Chapter Five, Peace — Blue, placid, peaceful, comforting
Chapter Six, Trusting — Pink, a shade of red or purple, trusting in His kingship
Chapter Seven, Cause and Effect — Purple, royalty, His sovereignty
Chapter Eight, Tempered Steel — Orange, the glow of steel in the fire
Chapter Nine — Victory — Yellow, joy!
Chapter Ten, Epilogue — also Gray, the future, seen "through a mirror, dimly"

CHAPTER ONE
Beginnings

In March of 1932, the worst storm in Ozarks history swept across Joplin, Missouri. First, a coat of ice sheeted the landscape. Then high winds blanketed the mining town with eighteen inches of snow.

My mother, Odessa Talbert, was within two days of delivering her first child — me. Because of the winter storm that promised to continue raging, Mother was taken to the hospital early to be sure she arrived safely. My dad, Carl Talbert, called his sisters and his mother to come to Joplin from Columbia, Missouri, roughly 200 miles to the north, to be with him and Mom.

On "the day," tension and anticipation filled the waiting room. Then, after hours of waiting, through the door strode Dad, his strength and control of the situation very much in evidence.

"There's been a birth — a little girl," he announced somberly, then added, "but she's dead."

He continued, "She's a twin. There's another one coming."

The waiting women were stunned. Dad continued in his matter-of-fact voice.

"Now, we will never speak of the one that didn't live. That's the way 'Dessa wants it."

That was so like my mother. She couldn't stand the thought of a child dying, so the family was forbidden ever to talk about my twin sister's death.

Dad paused in his announcement, then abruptly turning to leave, he said. "I need to get back in there, because the other one is about to be born."

The Talbert women would honor my dad's admonition. There would not ever be a word mentioned about the twin who died.

I didn't even know that I had been born a twin until I was fifty-four years of age. But then, that comes further along in the story.

Dad walked back into the birthing room. Later, he expressed regret regarding the great anxiety, the tense movements, the turmoil and mother's travail. The nurses, the nuns, and the doctors were quite concerned about the remaining baby who was also expected to be born dead.

At eleven o'clock before noon, I made my appearance in the world. When the nursing staff saw me, gasps of awe rippled through the air. There was a "veil" covering my face.

Beginnings

That first veil I wore was probably a part of the placenta that broke loose when my twin was born. It simply fell across my face and became like a curtain, a covering, or a cloth.

Several religious traditions say that a child born "veiled" is blessed of God.

Quickly the nuns tore the veil loose from my face because it threatened my physical life. Ecstatically, they began crossing themselves and speaking with excited voices.

My father couldn't help but ask, "Why is everyone so excited?"

Mother Superior explained, "Any child born with a veil over its face is a child of God. She is special, and some day this child will be something unusual, or always be close to God. She is a very special child sent by God."

I can recall being told that, oh, maybe two or three times in my life. Although my mother and father would remind me of this, they never pushed me toward anything special. My family thought that it was a neat story. And, as it turned out, the legend held truths I would learn as I progressed through life.

As the years passed, I continued to ask questions of my parents about the film or the veil that covered my face and the conditions around my birth. I have had an uneasiness, a precognition, or whatever you might call it, throughout my life. I have experienced a feeling of incompleteness, of not being consistently and totally present.

This void was remarkably filled when I learned as an adult that I had been born a twin. There is another part of me, my identical sister, who had not survived. With this knowledge, I came to understand the roots of my mother's unusual request — and her secret regret.

Earlier, Mother had been told she had an abdominal fibroid tumor the size of a grapefruit and could not have children. With her particular determination, she replied, "Yes, I will!" and left the doctor's office.

Indeed, a few years later, she became pregnant with my sister and I.

I believe my mother internalized great guilt when one of her twin babies died. I think she felt that it was because of her inordinate stubbornness that she became pregnant. And so, while there was ecstasy in cradling her live baby daughter, she could not stand feeling she was part of the cause of the death of the baby sister.

Yet it was not really her stubbornness, but the tumor that did the damage. Somehow, I feel certain that my little twin lay between the tumor and myself.

Later, with a smile, my aunt would tell me that I "pushed my sister out." In time, the thought came to me, She came first — and for many years, I thought I was first-born and first in life. In a larger reality, I wasn't first in either. But I now realize the source of my mother's need for secrecy. Because of her guilt feelings, my twin sister's birth and death were not to be mentioned. And I understand.

Revelations

Things decided in the dark have a way of coming to light, often in the most unexpected way.

When I turned fifty-four, my husband George and I planned a Caribbean cruise. By this time, my mother was in a nursing home with Alzheimer's Disease. My father, his mother, and one sister had died in the years before. Only my dad's younger sister survived.

Because of the upcoming cruise, I began searching for birth certificates. Mine could not be located. I sent to Jefferson City, Missouri, for a duplicate copy. When it arrived, it read, "a twin birth." I was dumbfounded. Could it be a mistake? This revelation was hard to believe. What had happened?

It didn't bother me that Mother hadn't told me. I understood my mother well enough. I knew she must have had her reasons. I could hardly wait to talk with my one living aunt.

When I questioned Aunt Clara about my birth, she avoided the issue entirely, saying, "I'm not going to tell you. Your father said that it was never to be spoken of. I am not going to speak of it now because your mother can't say anything because her mind is gone, and I'm going to honor her wish."

I thought, Oh brother! It took me about a year to convince my aunt to speak of the secret twin birth. But I was determined to learn the truth and went about my quest.

Before the end of that year, I traveled to Columbia one weekend to give a talk, as I frequently do for women in the Methodist church. While there, I called my aunt and suggested that she drive down to Columbia from nearby Bowling Green. I proposed that we could have a family time with the three cousins who lived in Columbia. She agreed.

We were all having a joyful time, because it had been three or four years since we had been together.

Then, "out of the blue," in jovial tones and with a wide smile, I "innocently" asked, "Aunt Clara, why don't you tell us about my being a twin?"

My cousins shrieked, "What?!" with surprise. And Aunt Clara loved the fact that she knew something they didn't.

With pent-up emotions held in rein for over a half century, the secrets were revealed. Auntie couldn't get it out fast enough. She told us my unborn sister had grown to be two and a half pounds while I weighed in at six and a half pounds.

What a neat feeling this revelation was. I now felt whole. But did my twin have a name? I wanted to know. And where is she buried? Hmm-m-m. More to learn.

Veils, Vales, and Vails

Returning for a moment back to my birth and the veil, a common meaning of removing a veil is associated with excitement, hope, and promise, as when a groom lifts his bride's veil to view with new clarity the beauty of the future.

As I pondered the significance of the word veil, two similar sounding words came to mind: vale and vail. Beyond that similarity, the literal and metaphoric definitions of *veil, vale* and *vail* hold unique life meanings.

A vale experience seems to be a threatening situation or event. These hold possible danger. The vale times in my life often find me literally on my spine and totally in a psychologically frightening situation. It is from such a geophysical vale position that I lift my eyes upward toward the horizon. Then, from beyond the outlines of the mountain peaks and ridges of my mind, comes my intervention in human suffering.

Intervention comes only when we are in the vale. There we finally have the opportunity to look up, think up, reach up, and say, "My God. My God, Jesus, Jesus..."

And He is there.

The geophysical qualities of each vale catches our attention because, physically, we are threatened. From these positions of weakness, we gain an understanding of the strength of the Creator. In contrast to the mountain top experiences, where humans feel all powerful, vale experiences can bring a deeper understanding of power beyond this temporal and spatial place. You realize there is more than just yourself. Through unusual ways, God will grip our attention.

And so, with a sense of fulfillment and joyful anticipation, I bring you my valley memories. They are a personal message from me to you, reaffirming the importance of our Eternal Friend.

The final word in our trilogy is "vail." Several spiritual meanings are ascribed to the word vail or travail. Where there is a possibility for travail, there are positive opportunities for God's grace.

The hardest part for me has been the humbling of self and the sublimation of pride. This includes kneeling for His great mercy, the yielding of my person, and submission to a higher plan. With practice, I have learned how easy it is to yield and to submit to God and to serve.

After I have been through the vale, and when a veil of darkness is torn aside, I can see the higher truth about vail. You might ask how my encounters with "veil, vail, and vale" would apply to your life.

Beginnings

My life experiences have shown me His unfathomable caring — His ultimate love, His strength and His power which is available for all of us.

During every vale experience, by God's wonderful grace (unmerited favor), we have the possibility of becoming stronger by reaching through and tearing aside the veils or hindrances to our journey. Through the vail experiences, we finally arrive where we should be standing, but in obedience, on our knees, in humility, joy, and worshipful awe of the faithfulness of our Creator.

I've given much thought to the writing of this book and its purpose. Why do I sense this strong need to share some very personal issues and events that have both challenged and enriched my life?

First of all, this book is to be a tribute to the grace of God. His unspeakable gift to us.

Furthermore, I greatly desire to share my walk with God with those who also seek a deeper spiritual comprehension of "the way things are."

I hope you will take joy in this walk together with me, for, as I tell it, I am aware that I will experience it all anew. And that in doing so, my own faith, trust and beliefs will be strengthened.

My hope is that you, too, will be encouraged to pick up your own spiritual ball and carry it further. And that through your enriched persona, others will be touched.

CHAPTER TWO
Holy Communications

"Jan, Jan, what have you taught your boys?!"

I remember "hearing" that exclamation as clearly as if it were only yesterday. Yet, when I look at my notes, it was thirty-two years ago. That particular communication was overwhelming.

Fear was the issue. Through my example, I had taught my sons Steve and Dave to run away, rather than to head off fear, or face it. Now I know we have to learn how to go straight toward what we fear most in order to overcome it.

My story begins during my senior year (1953-1954) in college. When I was suffering from a persistent case of bronchitis, my doctor prescribed a new drug. I reacted to it with severe side effects. Suddenly my happy-go-lucky personality turned into an extremely anxiety-ridden disposition.

I constantly wondered what was wrong with me. Psychiatry in the 'fifties was viewed with suspicion, so Mom and I felt we had to sneak over to seek help from a psychiatrist. He respected our concerns and maintained his professional ethics, not letting anyone know we had visited him. My, how times have changed! Today, you are nobody unless you have gone to a "therapist" sometime during your life.

After talking at some length with me, the doctor said, "Jan, you are all right. What this chemical reaction did was to put fear in your mind. You possess an anxiety of being alone with anyone. Your oppressive fears suggest to you that you might kill them."

Now, I realize this is far out. The doctor continued, "It's the drug reacting on your mind. It is my professional opinion that you will get over this. It may take a week, a month, or it may take a year. Sadly, there have been some cases in which the person did not get over it."

On returning home, I was filled with anger. I was angry at God. Here I had been the "good girl" in college—no smoking, no drinking, no carousing around. Just doing what is "right" and suddenly I was laid low with a load of anxieties and fears.

I took to my bed for three weeks to rest,

but my mother was just fantastic. She simply said, "All right, this is something that we can unlearn."

Using the wisdom handed down from her grandmother, my mother continued, "Jan let's memorize verses from the Bible. We will memorize good statements, then whenever you have these anxious, fearful feelings and thoughts, you will be able to say, 'I refuse these thoughts.' In their place you can say, 'I can do all things through Christ who strengthens me.' *(Philippians 4:13)* Or when times are really fearful, just simply say His name, 'Jesus, Jesus, Jesus.'"

After three weeks of working through my anger and finally getting my physical rest, I returned to college. Privately, I began to work on my fears.

Now, I never told my mother that I was having these anxiety thoughts every five seconds. I didn't want her to be frightened. She never knew. God is the only one who knew how often fear impinged on my being. But, at the end of a month, I knew that God and I were going to win eventually.

Audible Communications

"Jan, Jan, what have you taught your sons?!" was really my first direct communication from God. Then, ten years after the first metabolic complications, as a young mother and wife, I found myself running internally from my fearful thoughts. The oppression and hints of compulsion had been gone for a decade. But they—and I —were running again.

How was I going to face them? What had I learned through my mother? In desperation, I stopped, thought, and remembered her words. I faced them earlier this time. And again, together with God, we overcame this irrationality.

My thoughts ran like this: "Okay, God, what's the very worst thing that can happen? Okay, I can go crazy. I can be insane. I can be a person who is not trustworthy to be around her children. Do I have a choice? Or am I pre-destined for a life of torment?"

Well, I know that alienation from my family was not God's perfect plan. My soul deeply loved and cared for my husband George and sons Steve and Dave. Yet, the fears that taunted and mocked me tried to make me unfaithful to being created in the image of God.

In contrition and obedience, I fell on my knees. From the vale of despair, I uttered a modern day Job's prayer: "Okay, okay, that's it, God. Even if it means that you want me to go insane, I accept it. Your will be done, not mine."

I arose from my knees, this time *really*

healed, from the inside out. I finally let go and allowed God to be in control of all of me. I truly began to realize that God is omnipotent and omnipresent. God is to be first and foremost in my existence. For ten years, I had managed my mutinous mind pretty doggoned well. But it was not until I truly let go that I was *healed*.

Dreams and Voices in the Night

Further personal communication from the Lord through the years frequently came in the form of dreams. These dreams have manifested distinct symbolism, metaphor, even allegory.

One of my favorite dreams from God awakened my senses to a little brown donkey. He had the sweetest little brown eyes. And he was a very short donkey. In fact, he only came up to my waist.

In my dream, the donkey comes to me, lays his head right on my chest, and says "Jan, you and I know the truth. Truth is God. In that fact, 'truth is God,' fear not." What an amazing thing to say.

Dear reader, do you remember the "voices in the night" story of Samuel and Eli?

In the middle of one winter night, while my husband and I were attending a retreat at the Lake of the Ozarks, I heard God speak my name in an audible voice: "Jan."

I quickly sat up and looked around trying to locate the source of sound.

"George, did you call my name?"

"No," muttered my husband.

"Did you hear it?" I implore.

"No!" the sleepy, now gruff voice responded.

I told George, "It's all right. It's the voice of God. Go on back to sleep. I'll wait for Him to talk to me." Not another word came from God that night.

The following morning, we returned to our home church, Schweitzer United Methodist in Springfield, Missouri. As a part of our service and devotion to God, we sing in the chancel choir. George sang bass and I sang tenor. On that first morning back at our church, we sang a new song. The chorus of that song reinforced the meaning of my experience the night before: "...I will call your name in the night..."

As tears welled up in my eyes, I silently told the Lord, I'm listening. What do you want? I'm listening. I felt the answer was His peace.

Another dream emerged not too long ago. In fact, it happened shortly before our son Dave died:

Although it is early in the year 1991, my dream portrays George, our sons, and me in an earlier period. Steve and Dave are nine and seven. We walk into Schweitzer Church.

As we enter through the glass doors, to our right hand side we see a coffin — a gorgeous open coffin. Emanating from it, illuminating the space above it is the most holy, brilliant, beautiful, white light. The sight of it immerses me in a feeling of glorious, overwhelming beauty and joy; there is a keen sense of God's wisdom and knowledge present. And I am again enfolded in His wonderful peace.

The Dickensheet foursome continues walking down the aisle, turns to the left, and sits down. Presently, the minister walks out from the left side of the altar. He is a look-alike of our oldest son, Steve. At this time, I interpret him to be either Steve or his look alike — Steve's son Kelby.

Recently, a deeper interpretation of that dream seemed even more significant. It had to do with the passage of time — a metaphor of our Past, Present and future.

First, the dream took place in our family's past, with our children united at Schweitzer.

Then the present-time dream of 1991 portended the imminent death of our son with cancer. Dave's time of departure is near.

Finally, the future came toward us in the potential person of Steve's son, Kelby, who is the complete look-alike of his daddy. Only in this dream, Kelby was grown.

Through unusual dreams, God has had

His ways of communicating with me. These Holy Communications (as I call them) have given me spiritual insights. All through my life, in different ways, God has shown me He wants to communicate with us.

Late in 1986, George picked up the telephone to hear Dave's urgent but steady voice. The physicians at Kansas University Medical Center had just diagnosed the cancer in his leg. He and his future wife Terri, who are just about to announce their engagement to be married, have decided to postpone it until he can walk down the aisle. George and I talk, listen and ponder many things in our minds and hearts.

Shortly afterwards, as I sat on one of our church's choir pews, my attention was drawn to the back of the sanctuary. On the right back wall there was a brilliant light. The brilliance of it almost took my breath away:

Suddenly I am not in my body, but out of it... looking down at it.

I hear God say, "Jan, it will be all right."

In awe and humility, I say, "God, I know it's you. I hear you. But my sons and my husband, they don't hear you. They will think this is part of my imagination. Can you do something Lord? Can you do something that can prove to them that this is really from you?"

The next thing I knew my spirit had re-entered my body. The energy flowing through me was so palpable that I looked downward to the floor, expecting to see a pool of something all around my feet. It felt like warm blood, warm water, or warm, soothing oil. Of course, there wasn't anything. But the all wise God simply said, "That was your fear I've taken your fear, and now I've shown you my promise that all will be all right."

Then I understood what had happened. And through the warm, flowing energy sent by God, my fears for the future were banished. God had given me hope: it *would* be all right.

As we in the choir marched out of the sanctuary, an acquaintance came close to me and took hold of my arm. She whispered in my ear, "Jan, Jan, it will be all right." Spontaneous laughter rolled gently from my lips. My friend looked at me in bewilderment.

With a smile, I explained, "You couldn't know it, but you are a part of God's plan. He has just reaffirmed what He has told me through your voice. Thank you for sharing that. Things *will* be all right."

Written Communication

As an act of obedience, beginning in January, 1987, every morning as I begin the day, I now sit down, think, and write notes. These relate to thoughts received from God. Currently, I have seven notebooks containing His communications to me. I believe this book is one of them, dear reader, for you.

During these times of reflection and communication, an admonition came to mind that: I am supposed to write down the words of God's wisdom; I am to abide in God's time; I am to abide in God. His exhortation is to "Lift the WORD."

My attention was captured by the word "abide." Abide? Uh-*hmm*. I should look up the meaning of "abide?" In silent protest I thought, But, I know what "abide" means!

Suddenly, both within and around me, there was a deafening quietness.

Then it hit me: If I don't look up the word "abide," there will be no more very special thoughts — no more Communication.

So I opened the dictionary and looked up the word abide.

The first definition was that of being somewhere and waiting. I already knew that. Then my eyes fell on a second definition— *waiting expectantly*.

Tears trickled down my cheeks. How beautiful! God wanted me to abide. He wants me to wait *expectantly*. Both faith and hope are embodied in that phrase. "Wait...expectantly."

I thought of God's revelation of Himself to Moses: "I AM." And I knew that I am to recognize and know that God is God. He is in charge. He is taking care of you and me. I am to know that we are involved with God's power and guidance. My circumstances can be trusted to His hands. *It will be all right.* I am to be faithful and wait expectantly. I am to abide.

I remember this particular Communication because only two or three weeks later we received another telephone call from Dave. He was facing a bout of chemotherapy and surgery.

But the coming physical pain and discomfort were not the purpose of the call. With a sense of foreknowledge and urgency, Dave implored, "Mom, I want you to come up to Kansas City and stay for about a week. I need you to recount all you know and all you remember about all your special times with God.

"I want to be wrapped up in God. It is the spiritual part I need to know. God has given me a wonderful chance to live His will. I know He has called me. He knows that I can do it. I want to do it better than anyone has ever done it.

"Please, Mom, can you come and share how you have learned to listen to God? I need to know how you learned to make Him your Friend. I want to learn how to feel comfortable and be at peace with Him. Because *I* want to be that way, too. When God speaks, I want to respond in the very best way I can."

And so I went.

Becoming a spiritual mentor to my son became my primary goal. Missouri Highway 13 between Springfield and Kansas City was well-traveled as I shared my faith and my special times with the Lord with my son. Some were things I had never uttered before.

Melodious Communications

In addition to impressions and audible Communications, God often speaks to us through music. Since 1970, God has frequently brought a word to my mind in a song or melody. Some are original, while others are rhymes and tunes learned at an earlier time.

In 1970, the song "*Alive in the Spirit*" was given to me by the Lord to write.

In 1980, as my grandmother lay dying in Joplin, Missouri, I traveled from Springfield to visit her. Just beyond Mt. Vernon, Missouri, I was taken by the view of a gorgeous, green valley that stretches westward. In a rush, new words, tunes, and rhythms burst from my heart and mind:

"*This is the valley. This is the valley. This is the valley where the Lord walked with His men.*"

By the time I arrived in Joplin, four verses and a chorus had emerged in a new song of praise.

In 1984, my song "*I'll Never Ask Why Again, I'll Just Believe*" was born. And just the other day the Lord sent the words to a yet another song: "*God is His Name.*"

In looking back, I think maybe these songs

were sent to accompany difficult situations in life. Like the Psalmist, I hear His songs in the night. I experience His cosmic dance in life's rhythm.

Considering everything, I have lived a wonderful, wonderful life. Ninety percent of it has been perfect. The other ten percent is spread over time and I realize that it is in these times that God helps me grow. My times with God have been worth every bit of the ten percent of pain and sorrow.

God's Provision

In 1987, God communicated to me that these experiences were to be a book. And that I was to abide—to wait expectantly.

"Share Me all through the years," was His counsel. Then, knowing me as only He does, He added, "Jan, don't *shout* Me. *Share* Me; share Me, my friend."

Again I defended, "Lord, I *am* sharing You," and quickly amended, "Okay, you want me to share more — or in a different way?"

He responded: "Our communications will be a book."

For two weeks in May, 1996, I sat prepared to write this book. The experiences were in my mind. I had given many talks about them. I could speak of them, but when I attempted to write them on paper, it looked ..."blah."

I reflected, What is it I have learned? To

abide — to wait expectantly for His provision.

I was looking for some sign of God's affirmation. During this time an unusual phenomenon occurred around our house. A pure white grackle with a couple of little spots on it flew among the maple and dogwood trees. Its mate wore the normal iridescent color of its blackbird family.

Each day, as I stepped outside, I saw the white grackle circling above me. It seemed to speak of the availability of the pureness (white) of the Holy Spirit to all of us.

I spoke to my Friend in our normal friend-banter. "Okay. Okay, okay. You're speaking through nature. You have made all the provision for this book. Now, help me. Send to me someone who can help with getting it done. Take away the block that I have formed so Your Word can get out through my experiences."

One week later a very dear friend of our family, Dr. Stan Burgess, became violently ill and underwent emergency surgery. Medical doctors gave him no hope.

Our entire church went into prayer for him and six days later I went to visit him.

He recovered.

The doctors said that he should have died on the operating table...or that he would be a "vegetable." But he had a story to tell of how God had healed him. Stan walked to the Gate. But God showed him that he had other things to do before entering.

The healing of our friend is closely tied to this book. One visiting day, Stan's wife Ruth and I went down to the hospital cafeteria together. For a decade she had been studying with an esteemed professor in Jerusalem, Israel. The emphasis was on a new way of teaching people how to teach themselves.

I started our conversation hesitantly. "Ruth, I'm supposed to write a book. It came to me from God. He wants me to write it, but I'm stumped."

Ruth knew of my journal writing. With a slow smile, she said, "You know, Jan, the problem is that you have three books in those seven writer's journals. You need to find the first one, pull it out and organize it. I can help you with that."

Excitedly, she began drawing a matrix on the back of a used envelope. Then she told me to think of each chapter as having a color.

Bingo, it worked!

Since I had been an art major in college, thinking in colors made sense to me. So I sat down and drew a jigsaw puzzle-looking design — and "waited expectantly." Sure enough, the appropriate color for each chapter came to me. But here is the symbolic, marvelous, unusual part: every time I colored a section the name of the chapter also came to my mind.

Thrilled, I said aloud, "Wow! Okay!" When chapter two's turn came, I knew it was supposed to be white. An apt name, "*Holy*

Communication," described ways that has God connected with me all through my life. Even through a white grackle.

I colored the next part green. The title was to be: *"Living Your Prayers."*

I thought, Oh!

When I got to piece four, neither a color nor a name presented itself, so I went on to parts five, six, seven, eight, nine and ten. All of this was revealed within a short segment of time as I sat there...waiting.

Finally, "Lord," I challenged, "I don't understand. What's the deal with chapter four?"

"Look at all the colors that surround four," He said, "and read them off slowly. Listen to what the chapter names are. Listen."

Like a bomb it came to me. The color was to be red. The title was *"Symbolic Ways That God Tuned into Me."*

Great joy rushed through me. There was form and order now. No longer was my mind like a tennis ball, bong, bong, bonging back and forth. Through form and order, my intuition and experiences with Holy Communication could flow. My cognitive blocking was gone.

God's venues of Holy Communication continue to amaze me. He reaches out to me through the Bible, songs, audible words, unknown languages and poetry. Also through signs in nature, impressions and dreams — even in the mundane.

Recently a scripture reference, *Revelations*

19:11, lettered on the back of a truck impressed me to look in my Bible. I had no clue about the meaning before I read:

"*I saw heaven standing open and there before me was a white horse, whose rider is called Faithful and True...*"

Thank you, Lord. Thank you for being faithful and true. And thank you for seeing me as faithful and true.

CHAPTER THREE
Living My Prayers

An Introduction

The Lord is my shepherd,
My all knowing and compassionate leader;
I have everything I need,
He Leads me in the right paths,
as He has promised.

Even when I go through the deepest darkness,
I will not be afraid,
Lord, Your presence and word are with me,
Your healing and protection encompasses me.

You prepare a banquet that enables me
to live my prayers,
Yes, divine provisions against fears, changes,
losses, sorrows,...
The non-believers can see Your provisions,
Your grace....
              ~ adapted from Psalms 23, Holy Bible

Prayers can be spoken, sung, painted, danced, read, felt through Braille, seen through signs around us, and uttered internally. They may be monologues, dialogues, or intuitive impressions. Even the birds and animals can teach me. See how the bird rises singing, hovers to protect its young, and makes a daylong "joyful noise," as in the Psalms!

Prayers help me come to an understanding that it is God who directs all life. Thereby, it has been through His work and my reflection on my life that I have learned to live my prayers.

Furthermore, these insights then enable me to craft informal prayers. Through these prayers, a fuller realization emerges of His continuing presence, love, care, and leading. And as I grow in my understanding of God, a reservoir of continuing prayer enables me even greater opportunity for living my prayers.

The Psalmist understood the metaphor of a compassionate but strong shepherd who looks out for the best interest of his sheep. In this chapter, God, my Good Shepherd, first provides a lull or rest period in order for me to acquire the strength sufficient to enable calm in the midst of the storm. God's sustaining grace and strength becomes an enigma to those around me. My divine charge is to let God's grace be seen and to help others.

Our son Dave's life also becomes a correlation of God's grace. I am chosen to be his "life coach." Our family story repeats God's provision and intervention in the human condition. Sure, there is short-term tragedy, but the long-term good is for those of us who have recognized God's omnipotence and omnipresence.

The Winter of 1990

Winter in the Ozarks can be stark, bitter, frigid or amazingly beautiful as the rain changes into sleet and ice. The silver maples, post oaks, dogwoods, forsythia, and native grasses droop with crystalline elegance. Then feathery-like snowflakes mysteriously add volume and weight. A breath-taking sight emerges — along with increasingly hazardous conditions.

Then the weather breaks. High above, sun-rays course through the brisk surface winds.

As natives to this area, George and I adapt well to these capricious weather conditions. At this time, our focus and conversation was devoted to the next day's dedication service for the new church sanctuary. Since our choir would be singing at the services, we were both full of anticipation.

Then came Dave's fateful first phone call, announcing his cancer, along with his plea: "I need for you and Mom to come up next week as we talk to the doctors. They will be taking more X-rays and more types of tests are scheduled."

Suddenly that Saturday evening became anything but ordinary. Shock and fear alerted our senses, but, feeling the need for friends, we decided to go ahead to a Sunday School party at our church, where we were greeted with both compassion and anxiety by those we had been close to for twenty years or more. Their constant love and caring were to last us for the next five years. They were our support group and gave us the strength to survive emotionally and mentally.

We spoke thoughtfully with our friends about our willingness to go to Kansas City and be with Dave and Terri, and about the dedication of our new sanctuary.

When we returned home that evening, the winter's cold entered into our red brick bungalow. Wordlessly we began to look through old picture albums and scrapbooks together. Dave's strength was there in the photographs showing him pitching in high school and at the university. Other pictures had captured his broad smile and that glint in his eyes.

Newspaper clippings spill from a scrapbook of multiple years of all-conference, all-district, and all-state honors:

"...Dickensheet turned in a 10-1 mark as the Falcon's ace hurler this past spring, including a win over St. Louis St. Mary's in the state semifinal-final contest. He had a 1.20 earned run average with 83 strikeouts in 70 innings."

~Springfield Leader and Press. July 20, 1978

How then could this news of cancer be true? Then I became aware of something inside me that very quickly offered reassurance: "It will be all right. Shhhhh, it's okay. It will be all right." And I was at peace.

It was in our new, big, church building the next day that I experienced my first out-of-body experience. God continued to prepare me, communicating calmness to me. Over and over He repeated, "Jan, it will be all right. It will be all right."

Expressions of empathy, sympathy, as well as love and compassion, encircled George and me as we left the sanctuary. It seemed there were two circles that intertwined; one was God and the other was me. I couldn't tell which was God when He moved in, through and around the circle.

Through and around,
He circled and circled,
and in and out He circled.
He circled in and around
and through my circle.
I couldn't tell when I began
and God stopped.
Or, where God began
and I stopped.

It was a wonderful, spiritually clean feeling. From the time of this experience, I noticed right off that my prayers were different. I didn't fall to my knees, scream, cry, or holler and carry on. There was no melodramatic railing, "God, where *are* you?" I didn't do that. It wouldn't have been me.

Instead, I spoke softly. "Lord, please remember my son. He has remembered You."

Each morning for two weeks, I just got up and sat very quietly. I sang my favorite psalms and songs. I communed with my God. My soul experienced a peace it had never known. God attended to my soul.

And new melodies and words bubbled into being:

Past false smiles and brave looks
I will strive to be your messenger of love,
Oh, Lord, work through me.

At the beginning of each God-drenched day,
Prepare me to show the Way,
By listening, listening to the cries and pleas,
Listening, listening
Listening to the cries and pleas.

Oh, Lord work through me – listening
Knowing that whatever is Thy will shall be.
Listening, listening to the cries and pleas,
Oh, Lord work through me – listening.

Kansas City, Missouri

Early the following Monday morning, George and I began our journey to Kansas City. Anticipation mounted as we entered Paseo Drive and made our way to Dave's place. Skipping a couple of steps, I bounced up to his apartment.

"Dave, Dave have I got a story to tell to you," I blurted out in my excitement. I told him about the out-of-body experience and that God spoke to me by saying "It will be all right; it will be all right."

With the corners of his mouth turning up, he raised his eyebrows and I knew he was with me. And God was with the Dickensheets.

During this time, my interpretation of God's words was that of Dave's imminent healing. But the reality was — and is — the grace of God is sufficient through the hard times, even through the dark valleys and the vale of death.

A new, confirming voice of prayer came into our lives while we were at the University of Kansas Medical Center. The day after we arrived, Dave's future wife Terri called Mrs. Happy, a seventy-year-old woman from the Randolf Methodist Church, to pray for Dave.

Mrs. Happy has devoted her life to a ministry of prayer. She was considered "the prayer person" in that church. Anytime anyone is struggling or fearful, Mrs. Happy was called. Then she prayed and meditated. All day long she would go to into prayer. Later that evening we received her message: God had assured her that it would be all right.

Meanwhile, the Dickensheets gathered inside the medical center. It was shiny and clean, warmed with muted colors. Shortly, the room filled with three noted bone-cancer physicians and their nurses. Each physician brought ominous news. Each test record confirmed the preceding one — terrifying findings: osteo carcinoma in the bone above the knee of the left leg. A hopeful, but not a positive prognosis is repeated over and over. Surgery is recommended to remove the diseased portion of Dave's leg.

As each physician reported his findings, it seemed the winds of a dark funnel cloud began swirling around inside the room. The gray, swirling winds made an overwhelming sight and sound. I glanced toward George, who was standing at an angle behind gray accordion-pleated room dividers. With each diagnostic report, George's body rocked — no, convulsed or reeled.

My thoughts raced: Is he is going to be caught up in this tornado? Or is he like a boxer in the ring — being pummeled by an overpowering opponent? Ohhh, he is in agony. Will he go down for the call? I love him so.

My first impulse was to rush to his side. Then suddenly I realized that I am becoming entangled with his *and* Dave's problems.

Dear God, dear God, I can't carry my husband too! I cried in a private voice. My son needs me. Please, take care of George. I know I must keep an openness to You so Your power and energy can flow to Dave. He must not see his dad's fear. Dave must see hope and belief. I feel like You want me to be Dave's mentor at this time. Dear Lord, please let Your love that casts out all fear flow on through me to Dave.

Dave, his left leg in a splint, was sitting up on his bed so he would not damage it even further. Terri sat on the bed with him. I remember focusing on them as the doctors told them the very worst things of his prognosis that you can imagine hearing.

Every time they said something startling, Dave looked at me. I was standing outside the main circle of physicians, but Dave and I were in direct eye contact. It appeared to me that Dave and Terri were now in the eye of the unseen tornado. The storm raged all around the outside of that circle, but I kept my eyes fastened on Dave, with all the peace and calm God put within me.

And Dave kept eye contact with me.

Throughout this time, George and Terri told me later, an unnatural peace came over me. They said my face was shining as I looked at Dave with calm, compassion and tenderness.

Dave smiled at me and, looking back at

the medical experts, said simply, "And...?"

"Are you understanding what I am telling you?" asked one of the incredulous physicians, and he proceeded to tell us about the devastating effect of the upcoming chemotherapy.

Again, Dave looked at me. He saw that I was still at peace. He appeared to sense the calmness — even a flow of joy — within the surrounding storm. Dave's smile remained steadfast.

After giving the diagnostic summary and a plan of action, the doctors and nurses prepared to leave. I moved toward the door and followed one of the physicians, a slight man who appeared to be of Armenian or Lebanese descent.

Catching up with him in the hallway, I said, "Doctor, thank you."

"For what?" he exclaimed, his black eyes burning. "I hate this part of my job. I hate this part of my job. I hate this part of my job!"

"But doctor," I countered, "you told Dave horrible things in such a kind, compassionate way. *That* is why I want to thank you."

The beset physician took off running the other way.

As I continued down the halls into a visiting room, a question in a familiar voice entered my mind: "Where are you going, Jan?"

"God, I have to go find a Bible," I answered.

"What for?"

I asked a rhetorical question. "Isn't this a good a time to look up phrases from the Bible to help me?"

And it was like, "Yeah, it's okay."

I spotted a hospital copy of the Bible lying on an end table. Picking up the Holy Book, it opened randomly to a page giving hope. This opening was so random that I have yet to find that exact phrase again. But to paraphrase what I read that day, it went like this: "Fear not. I will heal your bones and replenish your flesh." *[Since this writing, I have found it in Proverbs 3.]*

"Thank you," I said aloud, slamming the book shut. Then I walked out into the corridor with my head up.

Shortly afterwards, Mrs. Happy entered our lives again. She had been in prayer for the past eight hours. While praying, the location of Dave's bone-cancer was revealed to her. Yet, she did not have a feeling of gloom and depression about Dave's case, but good and wonderful feelings. She related that the Lord was very involved in this special experience.

Meanwhile, Back in the Ozarks

(We Can) Stand Up on Our Knees
We can rise up and be counted,
We can look up and be free.
We can speak for God and boldly
We can stand up on our knees.
~Jonathan Cooney (1992)

Later a good preacher friend wrote a touching and meaningful song, "*(We Can) Stand Up on our Knees.*" It is the title that means so much to me. During this period, I was "standing up on my knees," remembering where life power comes from. I faced and went forward, stalwart through whatever I would have to go through — but standing on my knees. I was living my prayers.

While at home during this time, I continued my professional counseling services. My counseling helped me to keep my balance. One client asked, "How do you continue to believe in God while this has happened to your son?"

My only possible response was, "I don't know why God allowed this, but how could I not believe in Him? I know Who is in charge, and that is God. Whether I understand or not, I do love Him, care for Him, believe in Him and have faith and trust in Him, no matter what happens."

In January of 1987, the black telephone rang. It was Dave, announcing that he was to have two months of chemotherapy. Then they would operate on his leg.

"Say, Mom," he said, "why don't you come on up? I've seen how you responded to God through ordinary and even through extraordinary times. Tell me about that part of your faith. Terri and I are doing all the rest, but I need my spiritual mentor."

Every time Dave was to have chemotherapy I traveled to Kansas City and spent a week with him and Terri. I felt the bond of a unique kinship forming. But there was more. It related to a divine mission that Dave felt he had been called for. He deeply loved the scripture recorded in Isaiah 43:1-5 *(Living Bible)*:

...Don't be afraid, for I have ransomed you; I have called you by name; you are mine. When you go through deep waters and great trouble, I will be with you. When you go through rivers of difficulty, you will not drown! When you walk through the fire of oppression, you will not be burned up – the flames will not consume you. For I am the Lord your God, your Savior, the Holy One of Israel. I gave Egypt and Ethiopia to Cyrus in exchange for your freedom, as your ransom. Others died that you might live; I traded their lives for your because you are precious to me and honored, and I love you. Don't be afraid, for I am with you...

I continued to stand up on my knees as I walked, rested and traveled.

Return to Kansas City

Chemotherapy. Dave was treated for two months with chemotherapy before his scheduled surgery. Following a day and a half of the devastating chemical treatment in the hospital, I brought Dave home. They hoped to save his life through this treatment. It took about a week before he could get his stomach normalized enough for him to eat and be strong enough to go back to work.

Every morning I sat at the kitchen table and meditated quietly. Occasionally, Dave would ask, "What's God saying?"

One morning, in answer to his sincere question, I had a definite impression. I said, "Dave, this morning He is wanting me to put my hands on your leg and pray a healing prayer."

Dave responded quickly, "That's all right with me!"

Well, the human part of me was afraid to do that. Uncertainty spurred me to consider, What if it doesn't work?

Dave seemed to read my mind. "So what if it doesn't work? Let's try it."

As an act of faith, I knelt down by the side of his bed. I put my hands within half-an-inch of his leg where the tumor was. Then I began my healing prayer, "Oh, mighty God, may Your healing powers flow through and around this tumor until it dissolves." And I continued to pray in this vein. To this day, I cannot tell you all the things that I said.

Then suddenly I was through. I stood up and said, "Dave, I don't know if that prayer was to heal you or me."

"What do you mean?"

"Well, I think God was waiting to see if I would obey him. I did!"

Thoughtfully, Dave said, "I think there was some healing. I don't know how much, but I felt something."

Two or three months later, while the surgeon was reading the new X-rays, he found an inch-wide white area all around the tumor. He couldn't explain what it was. He looked at me somberly and said, "I only know that it's good. Maybe you know?"

"Yes, I do," I replied.

That was the only time I talked with this high-powered doctor. Terri and Dave wanted to do the communicating. They were twenty-six and twenty-four years of age. They wanted to do it on their own. So George and I were always there as a quiet support system in the background. We listened to their discussions but did not participate in the decisions, unless asked.

I sincerely do not think that anyone in the room knew what was going on between the doctor and I. It was an ecstatic time within my spirit. (Even today I cannot explain this new relationship to God with others. Many in my family may understand this for the first time as they read this. It feels so good to get it out.)

The doctor explained that, because of the

shrinkage in the tumor, he now had room to cut, and not amputate, Dave's leg. Certainly the chemotherapy had helped. The surgeon would cut high on the thigh so there would be less of a chance for cancer cells to escape. First the knee would be removed. Then titanium rods would be inserted; one titanium rod would be placed up toward the hip, and the other rod placed down through the bone toward the ankle. The rods would be brought together at the knee level. And so it was done.

Boy, did Dave get good at walking with those rods in his leg. You could scarcely see the limp. I'm here to tell you that not one single cancer cell showed again in his leg. The leg was healed. Later, however, cancer cells showed up in his lungs. I believed with all my heart that the leg operation was successful. I still feel very good about the route we took.

There are times of wondering through most trying and traumatic circumstances. But I could see that God was totally, completely and absolutely in control. God gave me a precise table of processes that completely sustained me. Others began to assume that I was not dealing with the situation. I had not gone to pieces, as expected; rather I had peace. I had my God, and it was with faithfulness and trust.

Yes, God gave us five years of renewal. Dave fought valiantly. He held his head high, his bright eyes looked forward, and his smile displayed his confidence. He believed in his mission with all his heart, even unto death.

Dave knew he would be all right. So did I. George and Steve knew Dave was going to be all right, too, but they dealt with it differently.

As everyone watched Dave wrestle with his toughest struggle, they wondered that he did it with such class.

I am so proud of my family. Steve and George bonded as men and comforted one another.

Yes, as each of us lives our prayers, we learn to believe deeply and to be faithful to God. And, yes, we learn that things are going to be all right. You can prevail by "standing on your knees."

Even when I went through the deepest darkness,
Your divine provisions exceeded my
   human expectations...
Love, strength, and peace
   filled and flowed over my mind, spirit, and body.

I know of Your goodness and love;
I know it will be with me all my life.
I know it was with Dave, Steve, and George.
I know the House of the Lord will be the abode
   of Kelby and the generations who are afar off.

~ adapted from Psalms 23:4,6 Holy Bible

Ah! Blessed Lord...!!

CHAPTER FOUR
Symbols of God's Communication to Me

Symbols or signs in the natural things around us have been a part of God's communication to man throughout history. I think of God's promise to Noah in the rainbow *(Genesis 9:13)*; the bronze serpent that Moses fastened to a pole forming the shape of the cross-to-come *(Numbers 21:9)*; the dew on the fleece that confirmed God's promise to Gideon to deliver Israel *(Judges 6:37, 38)*; the dove above Christ's head as he came up out of the baptism water *(Matthew 3:16)*; and of course, there's the coming signs on earth and in the heavens preparing us for Christ's return *(Luke 21:27,28)*. All of these are a call to absolute faith in God.

I recall the symbols that God used to get my attention — letting me know that He was close by. Several times it saved my life. The first time I remember was back in the late 'seventies. I was driving south on one of

Symbols of God's Communication

Springfield's main streets in order to substitute teach in Cherokee Junior High School. I came to a stop light at the corner of M Highway and Campbell Street.

It was a very busy corner, people were driving into Springfield from the nearby small town of Nixa to work in town. A lot of junior high youth were on foot near the intersection, on their way to classes.

The light changed. The car in front of me started forward. As I got to the middle of the intersection, I heard the blast of a truck horn. As I looked to my right, I saw a double-load coal truck bearing down on me — and his brakes were gone.

To tell you how big that coal truck was, the top of its front tire came to the top of my Granada Ford. There was just no place in that intersection for both that truck *and* me to go.

All I remember was saying, "Jesus, Jesus" as I gripped my steering wheel.

Suddenly I realized my car was still facing the same direction and was still in the same spot that I was in before entering the intersection. Beyond me, down at the bottom of the hill in front of me, the big coal truck had come to a stop. There had been absolutely no place for the coal truck to go without hitting me. But I was still in the same spot.

The truck driver, whose rig sat in the middle of the road, got out, looked at me, and scratched his head. I just waved. He got back in his truck and went on his way. I went on mine. What happened?

I believe that time stood still and God took care of it in His own wonderful way.

I would have loved to know what people who were also in their cars at that intersection saw. Did anyone see anything? Did time stand still? I know that truck driver is not the same today, whoever he is. Certainly I am not the same.

I went on to the junior high to teach and I cried a lot that day. I explained to the kids why I was crying. I was very emotional because my life had been saved when, by all things possible, it shouldn't have been. I assured the kids they were not to worry about moments when I wasn't in control of my emotions. They were wonderful. They were the cream of the crop. Just great kids.

When school was over I made myself go back to that intersection. As I drove through it, I cried, "Okay, God, you've got me now. You will be Number One with me from now on. All of my life I've put my family first, then God, friends, and maybe somewhere along the line myself. If it hadn't been for you, God, and your supernatural way of saving my life, I wouldn't be here—so you're Number One."

From that moment on, I focused on trying to discern what God wanted me to do. I began changing my priorities around.

The next time I recall an experience like this was in the early 'eighties. One of my real good friends, a young preacher's thirty-five-year-old wife, had something wrong with her lungs. They shut down suddenly, and in June, 1984, she died.

All the people in our church had a hard time dealing with that. We all pitched in and took care of the young preacher and their two young kids. Then on Christmas morning, George and I went to their home and took their presents.

Our son Dave had given me a Polaroid camera, so I took that along and took pictures of the family and their gifts. Finally the preacher said, "Take one more picture for yourself."

And so I prepared to take the picture. "Move over here by the Christmas tree," the preacher said, "near the window." So I did. Then I snapped it.

I took the photo home with me, laid it on the kitchen table and began clearing the breakfast dishes. But every time I passed that table, God would impress upon my mind to look at the angel in the picture.

"Jan, look at the angel in that picture. It's for you. It's for you."

I said, "Sure, God."

I'll bet I passed that table five times, barely glancing at the picture.

Finally I said, "Okay, God, will you leave me alone if I look for that angel?"

I picked up the picture and right there in the left hand corner of the snapshot, near the Christmas tree, hovering right over the preacher and his two children, was what I saw as a little cherub angel. You know the little chubby, cherub angel. With those cute little wings.

I called out, "Oh, boy! George, I want to show you something!"

My husband, being the engineer type personality, is very logical and analytical. I told him what had happened. Then I continued, "I'm going to show you this picture of Clayton and the two kids. Will you tell me what you see?"

Well, two or three minutes passed. I asked, "You don't see anything?"

George replied, "Oh, yeah, I see something. But I don't understand why you only see one angel. I see two."

I thought, Whoa! This was heavy.

Then George showed me where he saw two adult angels in the same area where I saw the child angel.

David, our son who was getting his master's in Texas during that time, was home for the holidays. I quickly carried the photo back to the bedroom where he was. "Look Dave," I said in excitement. "What do you see here?'

Dave looked at the snapshot and replied, "In the upper corner I see a little cherub angel."

That was exciting. David and I saw it exactly the same. Everyone else I've shown it to throughout the years see the adult angels.

Not long ago when I showed it to a young

person, her response was: "What about the big guardian angel that's standing behind everybody?"

"Where?" I said in astonishment.

Yes, there is a light shadow which you can barely see. This gigantic image fills the room behind them. It is still so exciting to see that little picture with all that in it!

Meanwhile, on that same Christmas day when I snapped that very special picture, I took it to a real good friend of mine, Joyce Cloven. We have been friends for thirty years, so I knew she wouldn't think I was nuts.

I ran up the steps and, as I started to ding-dong the bell, I looked down at the picture. There was water in the eyes of the preacher.

I thought, Oh, shoot! I got water on it. I rubbed it off on my pants.

All of a sudden I thought. "Where did that water come from?"

I looked around and, although it was a cloudy day, there was no rain, no snow, no nothing.

My immediate reaction was, Oh, no! Is this something from God? Is this another symbol from God?

Then I said half-aloud, "Well, God, if you have a symbol here for me, I'm ready for it."

I raised the picture in front of my face again and I stared at it.

I know this may be hard to believe, dear reader, but stay with me. Two water drops formed in the preacher's eyes and dripped down on his children

For a split-second my instinct told me that I had seen just a flash of God's work — just so quick an opening and a shutting. It took my breath away. (Even today, when the film is held in a certain way, you can see the marks on the finish that those teardrops made.)

I said inwardly, My God, my God, how can a human being even survive in knowing what amazing things you can do? This little thing is just nothing to you — but such a big thing to me. The words that came out of my mouth were, "I'll never ask why again. I'll just believe, Lord; I'll just believe."

I went straight home, sat down, and wrote a song. Now the lyrics have been given to two or three people who write music. Each has given it back to me. I can't find the person who hears the melody to it, but I know at the right time someone will hear the music.

Currently, a nice young friend of mine, who's a music director in Illinois, has the lyrics. He understands when I say I can hear violins, French horns, and what we call "the pipe" in the lyrics. The combination of four or five wind-tubes bound together in one instrument produces a high, eerie, classical sound that is gorgeous. I hear this kind of music in the lyrics, but I don't know how to write it. So we will see.

But I do want to tell you this: Two years later to the day, (it was now 1984) Dave was diagnosed with cancer in his leg. Yet, I am

Symbols of God's Communication

here to tell you that not once during this time of walking with God during Dave's battle with cancer did I once ask God, "Why?" That day, after my encounter with the truck, when I sat on my porch and drew near to my Heavenly Father, was a genuine turning point in my spiritual insight. God showed me through His symbols what life, and especially life in Him, was all about. God's ways are so fabulous, so wonderful, so awesome, that I understood; I knew and I believed: God knows what He is doing, and I am not to fear. He was in charge and I was not afraid. It would be alright.

In 1988 Dave's cancer was in remission. He and Terri married, so I had a few months where I felt I could take care of myself. I had to face a mastectomy. But it wasn't traumatic; what my son had to fight seemed so much bigger.

I entered into a lot of peace the night before I was to have my surgery.

All of a sudden a young male nurse came running into my room, saying, "Boy, you must have at least thirty flower arrangements! In one of these flower arrangements is a cricket and we can hear it down the hall."

I said, "I think I know which one it's in." And I pointed to an arrangement that had come from St. Louis from close friends of ours.

He said, "Can I take the arrangement out in the hallway and look for it?"

"Sure!" I said.

Pretty soon he came back looking so excited. "Mrs. D.," he said, (I had been an old school teacher and that's what I had them call me. With a name like Dickensheet you don't always allow kids to get carried away. If they liked me they called me 'Mrs. D.') "guess what! It's a white cricket!"

"Really," I said. "I wonder what that means."

He continued, "When I was in the Orient last year I was told that the white cricket meant HOLY, and all is well."

"Thank you," I told him, then turned my head and said, "Thank you, God. There's another symbol of your presence with me all the time."

So the peace was constant.

You know, it's really fun to watch and to look for all the different symbolic ways God comes to you. Looking back, of course, it is a lot easier to recognize the symbols.

In 1991, after five years of battling cancer, Dave won the war. He went home to live with his Lord. Our whole family dealt with it powerfully; God was so in tune with each person in our family at that time. How proud I was of our other son, Steve and how well he handled his anguish over his brother. The next morning after Dave's death, I went out on my front porch. There sat a red cardinal, it was Dave's favorite bird.

And sitting two feet in front of me on the

front porch was a male cardinal singing for all that he was worth. He was singing and throwing his head at me, so I walked toward him, close enough to where the bird realized I was there.

"Good Morning," I said. "All is well." He sang a few more bars and off he went. I felt that was my connection and God's way of assuring: "It is well with Dave's soul. Now let it be well with your soul."

CHAPTER FIVE
Peace — Gathering Strength

It seems throughout my life I have been learning to believe before a thing is proven, to trust before it is seen and to worship before receiving. These are the ways of the Lord.

I am reminded of all the times of peace we were given during the turmoil of our son's five-year cancer battle.

It was 1988, a wonderful year of peace. Dave was well enough to get married to Terri on May 21st of that year. They were married at Schweitzer United Methodist Church.

In that year, about a month before the wedding, a marvelous thing happened in our family. April 8, 1988, we were blessed with our first grandchild. Steve and his wife Myra, gave birth to Kelby Drew Dickensheet, who literally gave us new hope and new breath, new faith and new trust in the Lord. What a joy for George and I to have this gift from God. Our little light, Kelby Drew.

Peace — Gathering Strength

During the calm times of my life, I have often wondered what I am to do. Am I working in the will of God — doing what I should be doing? I realized it didn't take trauma to be close to my Lord — that God was "peacing" me, calming me.

I am always given time to speak with Him. That's good. I remember the peace times of my life, the music and songs that came from the Lord.

In 1972, a friend died of cancer. I wrote a song that came to me, "This is Home...Black cattle on a green field, red brick sitting on a hill, this is home..." At the end of the song God calls the singer and over she goes. With arms raised up she says, "Ah! *This* is home."

1979, I was driving to see my grandmother, my mother's mother, for the last time. She was in a nursing home. Thinking of her, on my way from Springfield to Joplin, I laughed with joy because this marvelous ninety-three-year-old woman had left her earthly home and shut the door because she knew it was time to let go and go home to God.

She went to the hospital, but her body wasn't quite ready to die, although her heart was giving out. So the doctor put her into a nursing home; that made her quite angry.

When I walked into her nursing home room, my grandmother looked peacefully asleep. I walked up and said "Grandma, it's Janis." Thn I realized she was no longer in that old body. She had quietly slipped off with her Lord.

I walked out and I loved it; what a marvelous way to go. I'd be willing to bet when she got to heaven she told God a thing or two because, to her, there was no way she was going to spend time in a nursing home. And she only spent two weeks there. She was busy dying — concentrating very hard on God coming to take her home.

Between Springfield and Joplin, there is a wonderful valley just on the western side of Mt. Vernon. As I drove to Joplin that day, I suddenly looked up at this gorgeous long valley on both sides of the highway. The peace and beauty of it struck me and these words seemed to flow over me; I had been given another song to write:

This is the valley where the Lord
    walked with His men,
The Lord, walked with His men.
This is the valley, yes this is the valley.
And this is how they felt.
They had peace of mind,
Peace and support.
This is the valley,
This is the valley where the Lord
    talked with His men.
Yes, this is the valley.
This is the valley where the Lord
    talked with His men.

Peace — Gathering Strength

And the Lord prayed for His men
  "Oh, look around you and feed my
    sheep," said the Lord.
This is the valley. This is the valley.
This is the valley where the Lord
  rose from His knee.
"Send thy Holy Spirit, I asked this in
  my Name, my holy Name.
I go to prepare a place for you.
A place of rest and of beauty for you."
This is the valley
Where the Lord walked with His men
  and talked with His men,
  prayed with His men.
And it was good!!

By the time that I got to Joplin, the song was written and the music was in my head.

One of the "peacing" times I recall was in 1988, during Dave's third year in his cancer battle. I was doing dishes at home in Springfield and God tuned into my mind and said, "Stop what you are doing, get in your car and go west."

I did that. No one was around to make fun of me or ask where I was going or why. I was heading west when I got to Glenstone and Sunshine, a key Springfield intersection.

"Okay, God," I announced, "I'm going to the west city limits and not any farther."

I came to National Avenue, a major north-south thoroughfare, and looked to my left. There was the back end of St. John's Hospital.

I said in my mind, Do you mean I'm supposed to go to St. John's Hospital?

I sensed an approving nod within me. I knew the answer was "yes." Nothing was heard, just a feeling. I figured I could do that, so I turned left and pulled into the hospital parking lot.

When I had walked no more than fifty feet inside the lobby, I looked up and saw a young woman coming toward me, sobbing. I stepped in front of her and asked, "How can I help you?"

She replied. "I've been upstairs in the chapel and I've been begging God for an hour to bring me someone with the answer to the three questions that I have."

I said, "Ask me the questions one by one."

She did. Even to this day I could not tell you what those questions were. But one by one, out of my mouth came answers. At the end of the third question, I responded with an answer that I can't recall.

She looked up, smiled, and said, "Thank you."

I said, "Where are you going now?"

"I'm going back to the chapel and I'm going to thank God for sending you with those answers. Thank you."

She went back to the chapel and I turned around and returned home. I really was so excited about what had just happened that I probably wouldn't have needed to have gasoline in my car. I was just flying. I felt so good because I had responded to God's prompting. Without question I had allowed God to speak through me to give a young woman the direction she needed. I don't know who she was. She didn't know who I was, but we were both children of God. For that moment, we were to meet. One to receive and the other to give God's answers. It was so neat to be a part of this divine encounter. Thanks, Lord.

Living during a "peacing" time with God is a healing time, a time of getting more closely entwined with God's thoughts, what He is expecting of me, and what he is wanting of me.

During my childhood I came close to losing my hearing. Between the ages of one and five, I had ear problems so bad they had to lance my ears. I know it's hard to believe, but each year my ears were lanced thirty times on each side before I was six. There was no such thing as penicillin at this time. My eardrums were nothing but scar tissue.

When dad was an officer in the army during the second World War in 1940, we moved to New Jersey. We were close to Camp Shanks located in New York.

I was in the sixth grade when a teacher noticed that I liked to sit in the front row. She told my parents about it and Dad took me up to see the army doctor. During war time, they were the best doctors in the world. They had been "invited" by the U.S. government to "join up" for the duration of the war.

The ear doctor reported to Dad that my eardrum tissue was gone.

"Janis most probably liked sitting on the front row," the doctor explained, "in order to read lips more easily. I am not sure she is hearing well at all."

They had a way of testing hearing back then in which they would put you in a little room and vibrate a chime thing. You were to raise your hand when you heard it. Frequently, they would test two or three persons at a time. I quickly learned to raise my hand whenever someone else did, not when I heard it.

So I went through several years of reading lips and hearing slightly. The doctors said I was losing the ability to hear low tones. I rejoined the choir upon the doctor's advice—singing alto—to recreate my low tone reception.

For fifty-five years now, I've sung in a choir. And I have good hearing. I should have lost my hearing, or so say the doctors who have seen my ears. With nothing but scar tissue separating my outer and middle ears, they still ask me, "Why are you hearing?"

It's a miracle! I'm not only hearing, but there are sounds that send me up on my "tin ear." A high shrill pitch will do this, but I would rather take that kind of pain than not to be able to hear at all.

The army doctor told us, "Now, when you start losing your ability to hear low notes

Peace — Gathering Strength

again, just go to the next range — a tenor."

Well, I sang forty-five years of alto and ten years ago I began singing tenor. I could tell I was losing some of my hearing. But I picked it back up again and actually can hear tenor better that hearing alto. And I'm here to tell you I will *not* be going to bass. If I start to lose my pitch or hearing again, since I'm sixty-four, I'll not sing in the choir any longer. Praise God and thank God for that time of "peacing" he did in my life.

My peace times all through my life are when God comes to me quietly and says, "I need you somewhere. Come."

Sometimes I would get a phone call from someone who needed help, encouragement or support in trusting God. Other times I would be led to just drop by. I didn't know why I was needed there. But soon I would learn that they needed to hear what God would say through me. I would say simple things such as "Trust Him, all is well. Just believe."

The other person would simply say, "You were sent from God. I've been asking for someone to give me encouragement and to assure me that there is a God."

Praise God! it seems that these times only come through "peacing."

The day after the mastectomy in 1988, the doctor was to come in and take off my bandage, look at the scar and see how things were going. I remember saying to God, "You know Lord, I don't know if I can look down at myself."

My loving Lord said to me, "Jan, you are beautiful in my sight."

I said, "Thank you!"

He said, "Peace."

During these "peacing" times, information would come to me like, "wisdom is knowledge with God in it." The phraseology came from God.

In addition, I would also attend Bible studies where I learned more and more about God. Through all of this, the Lord became more of a personal God than ever before.

One more thing about my mastectomy: I read before my surgery that, if patients could go peacefully into an operating room and not have fear, that you would bleed very little and the healing process would be quick. I decided to try it.

Just before it was time for my surgery my son Dave came into the surgical waiting room and asked, "Mom, what are you doing?

"Dave, I'm 'peacing'."

"What do you mean?"

"I read not long ago that, if you teach yourself to go in your mind to the most beautiful place and reside there during the operation, that you would do a lot less bleeding and the healing would be quicker."

"Well, where are you going in your thoughts?"

"Oh, I'm going to Gulf Shores near Sarasota, Florida. I'm on the white sands close to that blue water near the Caribbean. And I'm letting the water come closer and closer. It's washing over my feet and over my legs and over my body. The water is receiving and taking all my fear. I'm filled with the joy of healing."

My son said, "Cool. Neat!"

As Dave whisked out of that room, in came the anesthesiologist. He said, "I heard you talking to your son and I loved what you were saying. I've worked with people like you and they have healed very quickly. So when we get in there I'm going to lean over and talk to you as I put you under."

I remember that in the operating room, the doctor leaned over and said, "All right, Jan, take me to your place of joy and calmness and peace."

As I was talking in this wonderful, relaxed tone, I went out.

Later this same young medic came to me and said, "You could have put your lost blood in a thimble. You were fantastic. It worked!"

Peace times find me giving talks about grief to grief support groups. This is within my licensed professional counselor realm of work. I began to be known as the grief counselor in Springfield.

My mind becomes very active at these times. Perceiving God working through me is humbling and yet exciting. I give various talks to support groups, not only for grief, but also divorce work shops. This extends to work with the Council of Churches of the Ozarks' humanitarian efforts.

In 1983, a devastating tornado rumbled through the west side of Springfield. Thousands of people were affected. I spent an entire year working with these victims helping with their insurance claims and counseling needs.

Instant trauma brings grief and also affects you physically. I learned a lot. From these experiences, I wrote a workbook for the Council of Churches. It gives comments and recommendations for what to do during post-disaster relief situations. All this came during "peacing" times in my life.

And that's when the song, *"I'll never ask why again. I'll just believe,"* was born, on December 26, 1988:

God touched my bruised spirit
  in a supernatural way.
No logical answer would surface
From my mind today.
So I'll never ask why again,
I'll just believe.

The act is so profound,
and yet so humanly impossible;
Gently and tenderly,
God made it the impossible possible.
I'll never ask why again,
I'll just believe.
The power of God's love

is too much for me to ken;
In this body heart and mind so used to sin.
No, I'll never ask why again,
I'll just believe.

Oh, precious God,
  enough is enough, you see;
Accept the doubts and fears
  of your servant, me.
For I'll never ask why again.
I'll just believe.

I gather strength for whatever follows During the wonderful times when I just sit back and think about it.

During one of those peace times in my life, in the early 'eighties, I wrote the following letter to the United Methodist Women everywhere. I wrote it from a child of God and willing servant of Jesus Christ:

"I wish to share with you an illuminating situation which I was privileged to experience at the School of Missions at Central Methodist College in Fayette, Missouri, on July of this year. The tight schedule we were on from six a.m. to ten p.m. at night, and then three hours of sharing afterwards, left little time for sleep. But it was so fulfilling spiritually and friendship wise that I had to write and share this with all of you.

You might be like I was this year, unwilling to take three days out of my busy schedule to go to the School of Missions. Thank God, I was led to go. One of our classes was on the prophet Jeremiah and his call from God to win the people. If they did not change their ways, disaster loomed.

In the class taught by Susan Vogle, there was a young woman from Warrensberg, Missouri, who was earnestly concerned about the role of women in the church. She realized that so often we are like the people of Jeremiah's time who were self-satisfied, lazy, and religious only when they were scared.

Eunice Carmichael shared a vision from God with our class. Full to the brim with the Holy Spirit as she talked, her voice was quivering and her body shook. But the Spirit was definitely upon her and the class felt it. We sat in a hushed atmosphere absorbing as much of her vision as we could. Eunice began the morning at five a.m. with an exciting part of Jeremiah and the reference to *The Yoke*. The following is an account she gave to the class.

She began, "My struggle has to do with the struggle of modern day living with reference to Hannah of the Old Testament and the appropriate life-style of energy and functioning as a mother and wife, and the yoke of total fulfillment in my Church. The vision began:

Hannah, a gifted woman, learned to channel her living at the various maturing levels of her life. At first, it was through prayer for

Peace — Gathering Strength

her needs. Then she brought her son, Samuel, to the temple to be raised as a priest. As Samuel grew older, Hannah made and brought a coat to the temple for him. Each year the style changed and the coat was altered.

Eunice felt that God was showing us here that, if we allow God to work through us, as we grow, our spiritual coat would need to be enlarged. Each year God has a different area of growth for us.

"Each year," Eunice continued, "as I grow a little older, God desires to fulfill His mission within me in an appropriate manner. As I go home from the School of Missions to my husband, children and church women's activities, I realize His fulfilling warmth is extremely important in a new style of circumstances. I pray my coat will be totally acceptable and I can, like Jeremiah, have ears to hear this call, so that I can grow in the maturing of what God is all about."

What a blessing this young woman was to me and to the rest of the members of our class. The years may dim her name from our memories, but never her vision, which she so graciously shared with us. The Lord be with you and your family. On behalf of the class, we thank her from the bottom of our hearts. Blessed are women like Eunice.

CHAPTER SIX
Trusting in His Promises

As I thought about chapter six and the color this chapter should be, the color pink came to me; the title, I knew, was to be "Trusting in His Promises." When I thought it over, since pink is a shade of red (God's power) or purple (royalty), pink seemed appropriate for "Trusting in His Promises."

Through the trying times, and various other times, too, God would bring us promises through many people. One of these folks was the lady in Kansas City in Randolph United Methodist Church whose name (I kid you not) is Miss Happy. I love that name.

She tried to find us at the Kansas City University Medical Center to tell us that she had been in prayer for Dave and our family all day and that God had assured her that *it would be all right*. The Lord then gave me some beautiful signs of God's promises to us.

I recall the double rainbow that appeared

to start above our home and go straight up and across about six miles in toward town, ending at Dave's home. I saw it as a double promise to remind me that God *is* in charge and God *was* taking care of things.

Once I saw the end of a single rainbow touch down in the field behind our house. Now I know why people say there is a pot of gold at the end of a rainbow — the breathtaking display of gold and yellow light splashing skyward where the rainbow meets the earth is a thrilling sight to behold. It tells me, take courage!

Then there was the day a young eighteen-year-old woman knocked at my door and said, "I need counseling and I want you to counsel me — and I want you to know that I don't believe in God, but it's all right that you do."

I assured her, "That's good because I *do*."

She sat down on the divan where I do my meditational work and looked up at the picture of a water scene that hung on my wall.

She said, "That's creepy."

"What's creepy?"

She said, "Why is the picture of Jesus in that picture?"

"What do you mean?"

She said, "Sit over here by me."

I sat down next to her and looked up with her.

"Now I'll show you where I see the face of Jesus," she said. It took up the whole picture.

From top to bottom. From the wavy hair, to the band around the forehead, all the way down to the eyes, where the horizon lay.

Floored by the sudden eye-opening, I said, "Oh, my goodness! He's literally been with me since January 1, 1987. That's when I began my regular prayer time with God to work through our son's final hours, days and years of his life."

I had sat under that picture for five years and never knew its secret until it was revealed to me by someone who said she didn't believe in God.

Once, during a counseling session in Dave's first year of fighting the disease, a client said to me. "How can you believe in God through all this?"

I replied, "How can I not?"

I just believe in His promises.

In that same year, I recall God had given me another promise when the bone surgeon showed us the x-ray of Dave's leg. It was before surgery, after two months of chemo.

I told the doctor, "I can't look at it, I can't look at that cancer."

Then God corrected me: "Yes, you can. Look at the white all around the tumor."

And there it was. The doctor was indicating the change.

"Now," he said, "I have room to save the leg." *It will be all right.*

Dave and Terri were twenty-six and twenty-four years old and they themselves and wanted to face the ordeal themselves — together. Of course the doctor worked with them. And George and I and our son Steve were in and around as their visible, silent support. The doctor knew we were there — we were beside them and behind them — but Dave and Terri did all the talking and made all the necessary decisions.

George and I felt God's strength and energy flowing in around us at this time. And, to tell the truth, it was a bit tough for us to play the support-but-don't-command role for our son.

In 1988, Dave was well enough for he and Terri to have a marvelous wedding. He had finished the chemo and had had his surgery and his leg was fitted with a titanium rod; he just didn't have a knee. But he walked beautifully, if stiffly, down the aisle.

After they were married, they returned to Kansas City to live. Then Dave's company, Enterprise Car Rentals, sent them to Springfield to open up an area office. And so now they were back close to us and to Terri's folks. And we were all silent, silent support.

Dave explained to me, "Mom, sometimes I need you to come and just be my spiritual mentor. Like every time I have a question, every time I need answers that I feel that you can give me because of your spiritual experiences, come. Terri and I will do the rest. We're bonded to do the rest. The only place I need you to enter in is for spiritual support."

And so time and time again I would share with Dave when God spoke or guided me or Dave asked.

Another time God gave me a special promise was at the time of Dave's death, when He said, "Dave is free at last from the burdens of the earth. He's rejoicing. *All is well.* Now go and be likewise."

A year after David passed away on his birthday, May 13, 1992, I was called to the nursing home to see my mother, who for the past eight years had suffered Alzheimer's Disease. Now she was at death's door. Mother's heart was beating but her eyes were locked. She wasn't responding and her blood pressure was so low it wasn't registering.

I took our associate pastor, Jonathan Cooney, with me.

Mother was so dearly loved at the home. The nurses, nurses' aides, maintenance people, laundry people — all those who had taken care of her and been a part to her life for the last eight years, were wringing their hands as we walked into the room.

I reassured them, "It's all right. You can go about your work; the preacher and I will go in now."

On our way into the room, I spoke to the head nurse. My mother *heard my voice*.

Now you have to know that my mother didn't know me as a daughter, or as Janis, for years, yet at the moment I walked into her room, she recognized that I was someone important to her.

I walked up to her and took hold of her hand and leaned down over her. She was partly deaf, partly blind, but I leaned over and said, "Mom, it's Janis, and *it's all right; I'm taking care of things* here. Why don't you go home with the Lord? And, Mom, look who is here; look around this bed. Who is here to take you home?"

I named her brother and a sister, her folks, and then I slipped in the name of her grandson, who she had never known was ill, "and there's Dave."

She opened up her eyes from this semicoma that she had been in, and looked over my right shoulder and said in perfect English she hadn't been able to speak in eight years, "Dave, Dave, Dave."

I looked at the young preacher and said, "Did you hear that?"

"Yes, I did!" he said.

"What a wonderful experience and promise of God," I said. "I'm glad you're here — there is no one else that would believe this!

"Now I'm going to lean close," I told Jonathan. "Mother isn't going to die at this moment. I'm going to take hold of this arm and Dave is taking care on the other side. The Lord has allowed that son of mine to reassure me, saying, '*All is well; it is well on my birthday.*' And he knows that my spirit connects and understands.

"Mother had to be close to death for this to

happen."

And Jonathan said, "I understand."

God communicated with me silently, quietly, and I enjoyed it, no words, no nothing, just holding hands with Mother.

My mother did not die for five more years. For thirteen years this wonderful, Christian, God-loving person had been in this nursing home with Alzheimer's. Yet, time and time again *God promised me all would be well* in that situation, also. And again His promises were true.

CHAPTER SEVEN
Holy Spirit: Cause and Effect

First, I must tell you that my hair stands up on my arms and on the back of my neck when the Holy Spirit is present. So I am very aware of it when He is around. It may be in a sermon, a song, a word of wisdom put upon my mind, or knowledge from others; it might be symbolic, in the form of a dove — or a white grackle.

I recall when I was five or six and lived in Wichita, Kansas. I had scarlet fever along with mastoid problems in both of my ears. This was before penicillin. I had been feverishly ill for three weeks. I even remember the quarantine sign on the door.

Mother put me in a snowsuit since it was around February. She sat me in a canvas lawn chair on the driveway on the south side of the house in the warm spring sun. To this day I can feel the Holy Spirit drenching me with healing rays from above. Accepting this joyous feeling even at that young age, I sensed something very special was happening to me.

Later on in my life at the age of twenty, when my spirit groaned and was touched by the Holy Spirit, I experienced anxiety, followed by peace when I leaned on the wisdom from God. Through the working of the Holy Spirit, I learned to trust His presence.

As time went on, I learned to recognize the Spirit, not only in trauma times, but in the plateaus of my life as well. I realized there was a time and a place for the Holy Spirit in all phases of my life. These experiences taught me to totally trust in God, for the Holy Spirit was a part of Himself, come to earth for all of us to benefit by, if we will. This occurred after God brought His Son, Jesus, home after His completed mission with us. For this I say, "Praise God."

When our sons Steve and Dave were in high school, probably ages fifteen and sixteen-and-a-half, I was leading a rap session with twenty of their high school friends. Peer pressure was at a high at that time. So our discussion centered around the fact that all things are possible with God.

I recall very distinctly that when I got home, the Holy Spirit faced me with something I shared with the group: the remembrance of my own experience with a drug-induced anxiety pattern.

My sons had not been present at the session with their twenty friends. My concern had been that the students would not talk freely if Steve and Dave were there. But I realized that the boys would likely hear of my recollected "drug" experience from some of these friends. Steve and Dave didn't know that story and there was the possibility that it might come out wrong or be misunderstood.

To ease my spirit, I promised God I would tell our sons all about it — if we were all home at the same time—four o'clock in the afternoon. I was in my early forties and still wanted our children to believe I had it all together. (I think we call this pride.)

Steve was in track at school and Dave was in baseball. It was in the spring. Both were practicing so I felt very safe from a possible "showdown."

One day in April it poured rain and both boys ended up at home. As we all sat around watching TV, I glanced at the clock. Yes, it was four o'clock in the afternoon. Suddenly my hair stood up. I heard God say, "*Now*, Jan."

I responded inwardly with a question: Now?

"Yes," came the firm answer.

I knew the Holy Spirit was in the room to help me.

"Boys," I announced, capturing their attention from the TV set, "when I was twenty, this is what happened." And I told them the story of my childhood prescription drug-induced anxiety disorder.

"When you boys were three and four-and-a-half," I continued, "I had a small reoccurrence of that fear and took you to Uncle J. E. and Aunt Lola's and put you two to bed with your cousins, Tracy and Tamara. But God admonished me through His Holy Spirit to bring you home again.

"Then I went into your bedroom without your knowledge (I thought) and fell to my knees in prayer.

"'Okay, God,'" I said, 'if You mean my life is to be spent in mental illness, I accept Your will.'

"Instantly, when I let go of control of my life and gave it to God, I was mentally healed forever. Praise God."

Yeah, they remembered that part.

But the important part happened at four o'clock that rainy high school afternoon. That was when I was privileged to show them how to put their trust in God and to share with them about the workings of the Holy Spirit in their lives.

Well, as we now know, both of them needed this information later in their lives — one to go to his Lord's home with his head up and with joy, the other let go of his beloved brother and finally accept God's will in peace.

That afternoon, after I finished my "confession," I remember both boys nonchalantly asking, "Are you through, Mom?"

"Yes," I said.

"Let's go play catch," they hollered jubilantly, "The sun is out!"

After they went out I cried with great relief; they still accepted me. I had not lost credibility. No, rather I had gained more.

My memories of the works of the Holy Spirit still amaze me, even though at the time I may have been unaware of what God was doing.

I recall my visit with Mother when she was in her seventh year at the nursing home with Alzheimer's Disease. She had not known me in years. On the way to the nursing home, I called out in agony to God.

"You know, God," I started out, "in the last seven years Mother's been just like a five-year-old child. And she speaks in this jabber. Of what use is she to you now?"

In the past, my mother had done so many things for the Lord and was a really stron witness for the Him to many people. But here she was, with her mind practically gone. She sat just constantly jabbering. Once in a blue moon we would hear actual English from her.

In my prayer of anguish, I cried out, "Why couldn't you take my mother home, and save Dave's life?" (Our son was in the middle of his cancer battle at that time.)

I arrived at the nursing home, and as I walked in, an ecstatic social worker came up to me and said, "Guess what?"

"I don't know. What?"

"I found the Lord! And your mother brought me to Him. I'm going to heaven for sure!"

She went on to explain, "I walked by where she was sitting a little while ago and noticed that she can still read the big-letter Bible. I couldn't understand what all she was saying, but she read it so beautifully. The inflections were there. It was just beautiful. I was literally spiritually touched and have started a new commitment to the Lord in my life."

And the social worker went on her way, leaving me in wonder.

In my mind I said, Okay, Holy Spirit, Son of God, Almighty God. Your way, not mine. My mother with her mind gone still brings people to the Lord. That is a beautiful plan to me.

From that moment on, I never grieved my mother's condition. She was doing what she wanted to do which was bringing people to the Lord.

Those of you out there who suffer being a care-giver to an Alzheimer's patient, let me tell you what peace it gave me to know my mother's spirit was still in tune and still doing its work, even while her earthly mind disintegrated. That's reality folks, that's reality. And that's wonderful.

Another time when I was conscious of a special work of the Holy Spirit was when I was on the front porch of a friend's house, getting ready to show her the picture of the angel that I had captured with my camera.

Real tears had flowed from the eyes of the preacher who was in that picture. In a split second, I saw something in that photograph that took my breath away — I saw the gentle radiance of gold, along with a white, ethereal fog rising from the river. I saw all that in a flash, then it was gone. The words that wove through my mind were, "Oh, even greater things than this can I do."

And then I thought to myself, There is no way I can survive in His world while I'm in mine. It's too powerful and all consuming. I thank God and the Holy Spirit for allowing me see what can be, if only for that fraction of a second. This just strengthened my belief, my trust, and my faith in Him.

In 1990, I went to the Methodist Conference in Fort Worth, Texas. There was a large "Happening," as they called it in the Methodist Church, with sixty or seventy bishops from all over the world and four thousand laity. Together, we were trying to bring back the actual feeling of the Holy Spirit in the Methodist Church. It had not died out; it just wasn't showing. We wanted more spark, more fire, in our form of religion.

When we signed up, they sent us information on two hundred different symposiums that were being given; the one that I had marked as my choice to attend was holistic healing. I thought, Yeah. God is going to let me be involved in my son's healing after all.

I rode down to Fort Worth with four

preachers and two other laity. When we arrived it was time for our different focus groups to meet, so about six of us were disseminated around Fort Worth for different meetings. I met six people at the bus line that would take us to the holistic meeting — I thought.

When we boarded the bus, the driver took off for somewhere in Fort Worth. I thought, Something isn't right. This bus driver is heading to the wrong place.

He dropped us off at a motel and started to leave.

I questioned him, "This isn't it. Why don't you wait and let us check?"

"Oh, no. I'm sure this is it," he shot back, and took off.

Sure enough, it was the wrong place. We were finally able to get through to the meeting headquarters and the organizers and ask them to send the bus back. But by the time it was all figured out, we had arrived back at the center and the day's meetings were over.

I thought, Well, tomorrow I'll go to this other holistic meeting. I'm not signed up for it but I'm going.

So I just walked the four blocks to Days Inn, West Room. (That's why it was so confusing to the bus driver; he had taken us to the west part of Fort Worth.) The meeting was up on the fourth floor and I was the last one to get there.

The leader of the group, who was standing at the door, directed me, "Since you are the last one, take the last chair back there at the back of the room."

I did so and shut the door. The leader locked it. Fifty of us looked at each other, puzzled. It got very quiet.

The leader quietly and calmly explained: "Listen carefully. Right behind those accordion-pleated doors where the lady just came in and sat down, there is a man holding a gun to his wife's head. The police are in there talking with him and they don't want us to do a thing until they come to the door. They will tell us what to do."

Whoa! Pretty soon the police knocked at the door, and our group leader opened up.

The officers said, "Follow us; we're going to take you downstairs the back way and come quietly. If anyone gets excited and starts screaming, we aren't sure what he will do."

Needless to say, we were very orderly going down the back stairway.

When we got down to the lobby, our leaders asked that everyone involved in the Happening go back to the center — that there would not be a holistic meeting that morning. We were told to walk close to the building as we went so that the man with the gun wouldn't see us if he looked out the window.

About half way back to the center, I came to a screeching halt in the middle of the sidewalk and I thought, Good night, Lord, this is not where you want me! Inside me I heard,

"Right."

Well then, I asked, Where *do* you want me? What focus group am I *supposed* to be in?

The answer was, "It's all right, Jan. Tomorrow you are already entered in where I want you to be."

I got out my schedule and looked down to see what it was. Imagine my surprise when I saw: "A New Way to Do Bible Study." My less than enthusiastic response was, Oh, Wahoo. That was not exactly my idea of how God was going to work through me to heal my son, but I was signed up for it and the next day, in obedience, I walked to that hotel.

Now, in Fort Worth there is a hotel called the Worthington. It is a gorgeous, old style, downtown hotel — a beautiful French provincial-looking building with a lot of gilt and plush carpets.

I walked in and went up the escalator directly to the meeting room and I knew as soon as I entered that something within me was instantly "different." Fifty people were there, waiting for the meeting to commence. At a place like that, I would normally bounce in and say, "Hi, I'm Jan Dickensheet from Missouri West Conference. Where are you from?"

But this time I didn't do that. I simply went in and sat down at the far side of the room. Only a young preacher sat in front of me; most of the rest of the people were sitting on the other side of the room.

Holy Spirit: Cause and Effect

The teacher began: "I'm going to read from Matthew and it's going to be the part about where friends brought a person for Jesus to heal. They couldn't get close to him so they put him down through the roof so that Jesus would be close to him and reach out and heal him."

He began to read, then paused and said, "All right, question one: What do you *see* as I read these Bible verses?"

Out of the fifty people there, twenty people raised their hands. He let each one of us say something, and you know what? Not a one of us said the same thing.

I went, "Oh! That's interesting." Now he was beginning to get my attention.

"All right, now," the teacher said, "those that will, what did you *hear* in those Bible verses?"

Twenty hands went up; twenty different answers.

"Wow! That's cool," I remarked.

Then he said, "Now those that will answer, what did you *feel*?"

Twenty hands — twenty different answers.

Wow!

Then the next question, "Now, what does God want of you?"

Suddenly a roaring sound filled my head. A wind blew from the bottom of my feet to the top of my head and back down again, through my body. I jumped to my feet and said in a loud voice (because the whirlwind within me was so loud), "My God, what do you want of me? You came to me in a dream two weeks ago about the little brown donkey who laid his head upon my chest and said, 'Oh Jan, you and I know the truth. It will be all right.'

"Then you spoke my name the night my husband and I were on a retreat one week later. And the next morning at church we sang a new song: 'I Called Your Name in the Night.'"

By then, I was dissolved in tears, but I continued to speak.

"Then a week later, down here in this gigantic spiritual meeting, the first hymn we sang was 'I Called Your Name in the Night.'

"I'll do whatever you say, Lord, I'll be whatever you want me to be. Just tell me."

All this time the wind remained at a high roar over which I was yelling. I was looking directly at the leader; tears were running down my face.

"Jan," said the teacher, "I don't know why God is getting in touch with you in this way. I don't know what this is about. But I do know what the tears are."

Suddenly, I sank back into my chair, exhausted. When the Holy Spirit has moved within you, it's like a physical something has been there and suddenly is gone. I felt as weak as a noodle.

The teacher said, "Touch your face. You'll

see that it is now dry."

There was no more sign of tears. And yet I could recall tears falling down my face.

He said, "I come from North Dakota. I've worked among the Indians a lot. What you've just experienced is called by them a "veil of tears." It is when God is so real in you and the Holy Spirit within you is so strong that this is an outpouring, a promise, from God. He is extremely involved with you at this moment. If you were of another denomination, you probably would have spoken in tongues."

I looked around to read the expressions on everyone face. It came to mind that there is a verse in the Bible that says, "and some will hear and some will not."

The twenty that answered all the questions had tears upon their faces; they had heard what had happened. The remaining twenty-five people sat mesmerized, looking straight ahead; they had no clue what had just occurred. It seemed once again time had just stood still for a split-second. (I think of God's control of time, and the experience with a coal-truck.)

As for the young preacher from Missouri who was seated in front of me, he said, "May I walk back to the Center with you?"

"Sure," I replied.

He took hold of my arm and held of it most of the way back.

I asked him, "Are you receiving healing?"

He said, "Yes. There is still enough of the Holy Spirit in you that it is radiating and I am receiving."

I didn't know what his experience was about. I just knew it was all right.

When I got back to the center, I looked up the preachers I had ridden to Fort Worth and said, "Listen, this is what happened," and told them the story.

"I need to get back to Springfield," I said. "Tomorrow, Sunday, there's going to be a revival at another church in Springfield. I need to be there to receive important information from the Lord."

They said, "We'll leave at ten o'clock tonight, after the big Togetherness, and the wonderful singing and the different bishops preaching."

I said, "Fine."

At ten o'clock that night, we were packed and heading out of Fort Worth in one of the worst rain storms they had had in years. You could hardly see beyond the front of the van.

As is common with preachers, they all just drifted off to sleep. Just the driver and I stayed awake as he drove. He asked me to help him stay awake, so we talked and we crept home. We finally got into Oklahoma where the weather cleared up for the rest of the way home.

We got back into Springfield around nine

o'clock Sunday morning and I had time to go home and eat lunch with my husband. Then together we went to the big revival at this other church. My husband George was going to sing bass and I was going to sing tenor in the 100 voice choir. I fully expected that the information was going to come from the speaker. A tenor got up to sing, and to this day I don't know what he sang. What I'm trying to say is that nothing in the service itself seemed to be what mattered.

Darrell, a young conservation agent who had ridden with us to Fort Worth and back, had been hearing God calling him to the ministry. During the trip he heard all my stories and we had talked a lot about what was going on within me.

While we were sitting there listening to this beautiful anthem solo, I happened to look over at Darrell and saw his face was lit up with a "white," holy look. Tears were flowing down his face. When the song was over, he turned to me and said, "I have a message for Jan from God."

Oh, that was the longest sermon I've ever heard. Afterward, I said to my husband, "Darrell needs to talk to me; he has a message from God."

George said, "All right."

So Darrell and I stepped over to the side of the sanctuary and he said, "When God gets my attention, He is going to be coming to me with some information.

This time the attention-getter, he said, "was like a big white snowstorm with big snowflakes. They would hit me in the face and I would be in tears. Then I would hear what God had to say.

Darrell went on, "God says to me, 'I have a message for Jan.

"'Tell Jan I will take care of her son Dave. She is to continue counseling, loving, caring and doing the work that I want her to do. I will be sending her people I want her to be involved with. Again, remind her that I will take care of Dave. He is mine."

I was ecstatic and thought, Oh thank you God!

Oh, how we read into things what we want to read.

That month, November, 1990, Dave and Terri flew to Hawaii and spent Thanksgiving week there for some special time. He felt awkward with his legs a couple of times while he was there. Then, one week after they got back home, he was paralyzed from the arm pits down.

Nine months later, I accepted God's way. I knew no fear. I only felt expectancy within me. I knew that there were about four or five ways that a person can be healed. God had made the decision that He was going to bring Dave home to himself.

And there was peace within me.

CHAPTER EIGHT
Tempered Steel

November 25, 1996

I've had to do a lot of learning — and tackled new types of education in my life: How to write books, how to get excited in order to express myself in more creative ways, and how to train the left side of my brain to function in an analytical, more orderly way. It's been an exhilarating time.

In this chapter, I'll talk about human interaction and take a look back through these chapters thus far. What I see is that, all through my life, God has been molding me. He has also been showing me how faithful He has been to me all through my life. And He has taught me to be faithful to him in return.

During this molding, or shaping, by the Master's hand through the years, I recall clients I have given professional counseling; I can remember being with Dave in Kansas City while going through the first part of his chemotherapy, and having a revelation, or whatever you want to call it, come to me.

On one of those days with him, I said, "Dave..."

He responded, "What is it?"

I said, "God is calling me to go home to Springfield."

I felt that he was well enough now that I could leave. He had been through some devastating chemo and it took about a week before he was back on his feet again and went back to work.

"Go," he smiled. "I'm fine."

It's okay, I thought as I drove southward the following Sunday. God had instructed me, "I have some clients that I want you to see. So I need you at home."

On that Sunday in Springfield, I received my first call; it was a girl that I had seen once before. Now she was on the brink of suicide.

Up to that time, I had always said, Lord, I really do not want to counsel someone contemplating of suicide.

But the more that I thought about it during that phone call, the more I thought, *Yes, I do want to be there* when she is making a decision. So I set her up for an appointment on Monday, the very next day.

A short time later that same evening I got another call. It was a young man who was devastated. He was beside himself and spoke through tears. "I understand through my mother that you will counsel me."

He went on, "I'm gay and my partner of eight years has left. I don't know what to do."

Here was another type of counseling that I really did not feel that qualified for. Yet, when I hung up, God told me, "It's all right, Jan. Don't make judgments. Just treat this like you would the heartbreak of a man-woman relationship. Help this person get through it. That's all you have to do. I'll take care of the rest."

Well, I could do that. I set him up for the next day, too.

A third call on that Sunday was from a recovering alcoholic. Inwardly I protested to the Lord: Oh, gee, I'm not qualified for this. I even whined a little: You *know* they always know more than you know — and they are cocky.

But, no, God wanted me to stop judging and counsel this man, so I set *him* up for the next day. So the next morning I had three in a row, at eight, nine, and ten — three types of problems I had never really wanted to counsel. However, it was "orders from Headquarters," so I knew I had to do it, and since God was involved, I was not really concerned.

The first one to arrive was the recovering alcoholic. He knocked on my door, then walked in and said, "My wife thinks that I need to come here. She says I'm very difficult to live with, but that's her side of the story. But if I want to keep her, I have to come for counseling."

He came in, wearing the cloak of Mr. Cock Robin, a very handsome man, probably in his mid-thirties, had the world by the tail. He could solve anything, do anything and he was "recovered."

I said, "Stop."

He looked at me in bewilderment.

I let go: "I don't want to counsel an alcoholic. You are probably smarter than me. That's all right by me. You think you know everything. You think it's everyone else's fault, not yours.

"You're here because God has brought you here. And God has told me I will counsel you, so therefore I will. But I still don't want to."

In my mind I'm going, Oh, my word. What am I saying?

He spent the next thirty minutes convincing me to counsel him. I saw this man every week for three months, then I referred him on to a recovering-alcoholic counselor.

My part in all of this became apparent. First, he needed to believe in a counselor and trust in a counselor. Then he could go to the one who was going to be able to reach him, teach him how to get past it and how to deal with it. He learned to trust me and then followed what I recommended.

You know, as he left that last day, I really felt sad when I shut the door.

"Oh, God, let him continue," I whispered. "Let him go to this person and let him grow.

Let him become a healthy man."

And God's thought to me was this: "Jan, you are opening a door for some of the people I will send to you. You will not know the ending of some of their lives, but without the open door, many wouldn't get the counseling that they need. You are an open door."

About six years later I heard from the young alcoholic's wife. She brought a book back that he had borrowed. He did go to the recovering-alcoholic counselor. Life was on the upswing and today the husband and wife are very happy together.

I said, "Gee, God, thanks. I don't always get to know the endings. It's really neat when I do get to know what happens!"

The next person that I saw that Monday morning was the young girl who was depressed and close to suicide. She had everything to live for, especially a wonderful mind. I wasn't with her very long before another counselor's name came to my mind.

I stopped her mid-sentence and said, "Do you know what I'm here for?"

"No," she said, curious.

"I'm here to tell you the counselor's name who will work wonders with you. I believe in you. I believe in this counselor. There is a good future in your life."

I gave her the name that had come to me. She left and went to her new counselor. To this day, things are looking up for this young woman.

The gay man never showed up. But I understood, because in this case, all God was asking of me was to obey Him. What a wonderful feeling to know that I had the courage to walk in obedience.

So now I know the ending of two people's stories, but I don't know the ending of the third one. However, I do know that God is in charge. And things are all right.

It's great to be a lump of clay on God's "potter's wheel." I began to understand that God is both creative and orderly. God has been molding me from the beginning of my time on earth. Slowly, through little things, He was creating in me the ability to trust Him.

Now, when God says, "Go and do," I can respond in faith. Over the years, his commands and my required actions have brought new learning and new excitement.

Tempered Steel. What a marvelous name for this chapter! I'm here to tell you the state of Tempered Steel is heavenly. It's wonderful. It's not hard. It's a joy. The color orange seems to exemplify it because this color is bright and cheerful. It's also the color of steel in the fire.

It was May, 1991, a month before Dave was supposed to die, according to the physicians. His thirty-first birthday was on May 13; his death occurred on June 22. This was another time when God was molding and guiding me. The steel was being tempered. I was learning to believe and trust in new ways.

Then, from out of nowhere, Dave asked, "Mom, do you know I'm dying?"

I looked at him funny, "Yes, why do you ask?"

Dave said, "You don't act it. I'm worried about you."

"Dave, let me tell you what I'm doing. Let me tell you what I do when I'm not around you."

At that point, I was spending eight hours a day, four days a week with him so his wife could continue working. Her mother would come on Wednesdays to relieve me of the pressure.

When I was with Dave, I was very upbeat. He was still working for Enterprise Car Rentals from his hospital bed. He was hooked up to oxygen, but that didn't stop him from using the telephone. This gave him a sense of accomplishment. The company was wonderful in cooperating, and this was a wonderful gift they gave him.

By this time Dave had been paralyzed for about eight months from the waist down. I waited on him hand and foot. And that was fine.

"Dave," I began, "when Terri gets here and I leave, I get into my car and I turn the corner. But before I start the car, I start yelling, screaming and hitting the steering wheel. I yell, 'My God, you are taking my son!' I will hit that wheel and I will cry and sob all the way home, Dave.

"When I get home, I go into the house and the first thing I do is sit down on that rust-colored chair. I hit the arm of it, Dave, over and over again. It's an expression of my hopelessness of not being able to help save my son. I can spout out all my anger, my hurt and pain to God, knowing all the time that He is holding me and rocking me. I feel it. And it's all right for me to express myself that way."

Dave said, "Oh, Mom that's so neat. But why do you do that so privately?"

"Because, Dave, the cancer is now in your lungs. You couldn't take me crying. So I did it all when I got home — and I had to get it done before your dad got home because he couldn't handle me crying, either."

I continued, "Every morning before I come to be with you, I stop by my good friend Joyce's house and I pour out my pain, my anguish and my hurt. She sits and listens. Sometimes she holds me. She has never said, 'There, there, it's gonna be fine,' or ' Now, now, don't cry.' No, no, she just listens. What a marvelous gift she gives me by just listening.

"And then, Dave, I can come here and pop in your door — ready."

"Yeah, Mom, you've been very uplifting. But what means even more to me is, you have accepted God's choice. You are doing it great. I can't tell you what that means to me."

For some time after Dave passed away, a really strange thing began to happen. In that first year after his death, I could feel God was still using this loss experience. Sure, I was grieving. Yet there are many things from that year that I don't even remember happening. Friends remind me, but I still can't recall those incidents.

I do remember grieving in the place of each person in Dave's life, other than myself.

For example, I grieved for my daughter-in-law, Terri. My grief bore the emotions of Dave's wife and lover who had suffered this great loss. I grieved *for* her — that what George and I had created couldn't last long enough for them to have as many years together as we had.

Then I grieved for our daughter-in-law, Myra. This wonderful person never really had her day in the sun, because Dave came down with cancer a week before she and our son Steve were to be married during Christmas, 1986.

Dave had taped up his splintered leg and returned to Springfield to be in Steve and Myra's wedding. It was understandable that people anguished over Dave. They were conciliatory and hovered around him.

But I ached for Myra, because she couldn't have the wonderful wedding day every bride deserves. And I grieved for her because she grieved for her husband. Steve, the oldest of the two brothers, and Dave were so close. They were best friends, as well as being brothers.

Steve's grief touched Myra very deeply. She had been concerned, thinking that Dave didn't think she was good enough for his brother. But Dave would have felt that way about any woman for his brother. It was not Myra. She was the one that Steve chose, and she was the perfect match for him.

I grieved for my son Steve. He had lost his best friend to cancer just nine months before. Then he lost his brother, another best friend, to cancer. He couldn't come to me as his counselor. Even though I'm know as the grief counselor in Springfield, I couldn't counsel my close ones. I grieved for them.

I learned that Dave invited Steve to come by their home two weeks before he died. The brothers talked alone and Dave helped Steve to let go of him. *It was all right.* That was another gift that Dave gave to Steve and the rest of us.

Although I still felt Steve's pain, I couldn't tell him. I couldn't express it. None of the family or close friends had any idea how I was agonizing with them — how I was feeling their pain. I couldn't tell them; they wouldn't have understood.

My husband's two sisters, one younger and one older than George, were very close to Dave. They, too, were agonizing.

They would say to me, "You just don't know what my pain is."

Inwardly, I throbbed, Oh, yes I do. God knows, yes, I do.

But I couldn't tell them, so I kept it to myself. And because of that, I did not really allow myself to grieve the loss of my own son that first year.

When the second year came, I finally felt free to grieve as a mother. It was on Dave's first birthday after his death in May, 1992, that I was called to my mother's side at the nursing home. It was then that Mother, in the final stages of Alzheimer's Disease, awoke from a coma and heard my voice. And that was when I told her, "There's your grandson, Dave."

I'll never forget her steady gaze over my right shoulder as she said clearly, "Dave, Dave."

I feel that the Lord allowed Dave to come back just this once to tell me *it's all right*. He was at peace. He has great joy.

I'm convinced it was another "tempering of the steel" experience. All the while these "fiery trials," these testing, refining things were happening, I still knew God was in control. And He is still helping me deal with the loss of our son. These tempering times are wonderful, joyous times. Every time I learn something new, I'm going, "Yeah! All right! I know Dave is at my right shoulder," like the great cloud of witnesses *(Hebrews 12:1)* in heaven who are cheering us on.

God worked in a different way through George; he dealt with his grief so beautifully in what I saw as a "male thing," although he himself seemed not to notice it. But I noticed it, and I tried to share it with him. And there was peace throughout the process.

It's been five and a half years since Dave's death. And now I can speak of my anguish, my pain, and my joy. Healing still flows through me. That flow has helped me to speak these memories into a tape recorder. Speaking them out loud seems to "unplug" the healing flow and keep it going. I feel that I've grown much more sensitive to others, and am becoming a more understanding, spiritual person. I hope others will benefit by my growth.

The final fiery trial in all this came with the sad news that Myra and Steve lost a baby before its birth just two and a half months after Dave died in June. Two years earlier, their son Kelby had been born. He is now a vibrant three-year-old who has brought happiness amid the sorrow.

And so all is well. Hear me in this "Tempered Steel" chapter, where God has been molding and shaping and refining me: What He builds will stand forever.

CHAPTER NINE
Victory

Chapter nine, Victory, shines with a brilliant yellow in my matrix. Pure joy! As I look back over my life, I see the path I have traveled was through trials, along with many good times, but there was always a victory. With this realization came excitement and expectation. And I wonder what more is there that I should be doing with my time here.

Reflecting while writing this book has enabled me to more clearly see God's guiding hand and direction year after year. I am really writing to you, my friends, in obedience to God's command to me to share my anguish, as well as my overcoming during the late 'eighties and early 'nineties: "Share Me, Jan; share Me."

God has shown me that he will need me down the road in people's lives. He wants me to continue sharing Him. That fills me with such joy. And joy is why the bright color yellow means victory to me.

As I think back, 1942 is the first time I remember knowing that God will send someone to help when a mortal steps through the pearly gate. You could say that they just step over or are "born into" the next life.

When I was ten years old, we lived in New Jersey where my father served as an officer in World War II. My great-grandmother and several other family members lived in Joplin, Missouri. At 90 years old, Great Grandmother had been in a deep coma for several weeks. My grandmother cared for her and told us of this incident.

While still comatose, Great-Grandma Mattie abruptly sat straight up in bed. Then, with great joy and a light in her eyes, Mattie looked toward the base of the bed and said, "Ollie, He's coming for me Himself. There He is — Jesus, precious Jesus. He's come for me Himself!"

With that, Great Grandmother Mattie lay back down and, with a gorgeous smile on her face, she went off.

This was a meaningful story to me as a child, and at different times of my life. This knowledge has been helpful when I have been present while someone was making this transition to the other side. I know that I can talk comfortingly with them as they slip over, and that eases the passing for them, and for those of us who remain. My son's transition to the other side was somewhat different, but

Victory

filled with God's peace and joy nonetheless.

At the moment he passed over, Dave and Terri were together. Terri had asked me if she might be alone with him during his last moments.

For just a heartbeat I thought, Oh, no, that's my son. Let me be the one. But of course I said "Yes." I knew that was what Dave wanted also.

While Terri was with Dave, I was in Dave's kitchen, looking out the window.

Suddenly God's presence was upon me; He said, "Jan, Jan, Dave's with Me now. He is no longer paralyzed. He's running and jumping and laughing. He is so excited. Oh, Jan, he's so happy. Now, go to his room and be at peace and know in your heart that your son is with Me."

Turning from the window, I saw Terri's father come through the kitchen door; he said, "Terri just said that Dave is gone."

I had already known it.

Thank you for all the joy, dear God. The joy that came when my son's soul went soaring home to meet the Lord. He is born into heaven. I knew, like Jesus' mother did, the instant her Son was born again into heaven to be with His Father God.

Terri told us that, as Dave lay in his bed, he was talking with Dave Mayo, a friend who had died of leukemia nine months before. He was Dave's brother Steve's best friend. Terri heard our Dave laughing and talking to Mayo. (We always referred to him by his last name.)

Our Dave chuckled and carried on and said things like, "Mayo, remember the time when...."

It was then, Terri said, that she realized someone had come for her Dave. He would not have to step across alone, but he would walk with his head up and on his own two feet. He had a friend beside him, showing the way.

Oh, yes, there is joy in this knowledge. Just picture it: Terri was able to lean over and say, "Dave, go on. I can take care of things now. It's all right. I'll make it."

Dave squeezed her hand and said, "Remember, life is good and worth living, and I will love you through eternity." And Dave was born again — with his Lord.

When I recall all of the times that God has molded and remolded me, would I have missed this? I think not. I would not have chosen for my son to die young, but I would not have missed being a part of it.

Dave's sojourn here on earth was for God. He was definitely on a mission — and he completed it. Even the fact that he left us with a joy in our hearts is a victory. These wonderful thoughts will be carried with me always.

God has many plans for me still. How do I know this? I know because he has me cleaning out my closets and getting rid of clothes

Victory

that I have not worn in a long time. Sometimes I ask, "Why am I doing this, Lord? Why am I preparing the clothing?"

God answers, "Because I want you to continue sharing my wisdom and knowledge that I bring to you. You will do this, but you must prepare to give talks. You must prepare your clothing. You must get organized."

I have heeded this message. I am reorganizing my life to make it like God wants it.

In 1991, when Dave passed away a neighbor gave Terri a Precious Moments figurine. It was of a young ball player. He has just hit a ball and laid the bat down and he is running for first. At the bottom of the figure it says "I'm coming home, Lord." I cannot tell you what a joy and comfort I found in that little figurine. What a glorious way to think of Dave: "I'm coming home Lord, full tilt. Yes!"

Terri took the figurine out to where Dave is buried and set it on the gravestone in full view. It stayed there for four years in all sorts of weather. Finally, perhaps due to a mowing machine, the little baseball player was knocked off and broken. But it lasted four years! And it was wonderful to be able to drive by all that time and see, "I'm coming home, Lord."

Yes!

Through reviewing these journals or chapters, becoming more organized, and writing this book, my brain has become "unlocked." There's a sense of victory and joy unspeakable, as well as a peace beyond understanding. My grief is on another level of healing. (What an interesting thought.)

We all have keys. Our challenge is to find the right one to unlock what God has for us. I remember saying, "God, You have to send me someone who will help me unlock my mind so I can get all this down." And He has.

Well, this is not the ending of my saga, or of God's revelation of Himself and His care for us. But there was an ending to this chapter of my life. It was when I experienced the greatest possible spiritual growth that I could have assimilated at that point. I feel similar growth is possible for you.

God really has plans for all of us if we listen to Him. If we sensitize our souls and spiritual ears, He will direct us. He won't always save us from hard times, but He will make them victorious.

CHAPTER TEN
Epilogue

This chapter is rather a summary, in which I reflect on the basic meanings of each of the chapters; and I'll share the insights of many people who knew our family. They felt our pain and observed our spiritual growth through the hard times, sorrows, and joys. They have been various kinds of partners on the path as we experienced our deepest or closest time with the Lord.

It is my hope that you, dear reader, might see parallels to these experiences in your own personal stories and gain from them. All our lives are composed of many of these accounts. I believe that the Lord means for each of us to release our life histories and share God's grace with others as part of His command to "go and be witnesses" and to "love one another."

We're not here, after all, just to roll around, goof off, cry, or mope. We are here to be God's hands, feet, and voice. For this He has need of us.

After re-reading the preceding nine chapters one by one, I became distinctly aware of God's total faithfulness toward me. All through my life — about every ten years — He seemed to make a purposeful effort to let me know that He was present, and for a particular purpose. In review, here are some of the lessons I myself have learned in each chapter of my life:

Chapter One, Beginnings

The Lord has been my Teacher, either through experience or through His *Word*, delivered by one or another modern-day disciple to this ordinary woman in the twentieth century. I realized early on that God was working in and through others, as well as myself.

He simply taught me to listen to the inner guidance and insights given by Him, then to *share the knowledge and wisdom* with those he directed me to.

I became unafraid to speak out my newfound information in the hope that others would more clearly hear and heed God's word in their own unique lives and personalities. Thus God's guidance and wisdom would multiply and spread in every direction. In this way, I learned how to be faithful to Him, as He has always been to me.

Chapter Two, Holy Communication

Communication skills are so needed in every relationship. The inter-communion between God and self (flowing up and down) and between self and others (across and back, to and from) form a familiar pattern, the greatest symbol of God's grace: the cross.

When I began to focus on Holy Communications, I realized how, through the years, God had instilled visual, auditory and tactile teaching skills in me to commute the importance of emotional as well as spiritual growth toward maturity. The thought that I could become an avenue through which God could communicate His Word to others — who would then pass it on — was ambrosial.

Chapter Three, Living My Prayers

When a puppy or kitten becomes in tune with his master, his eagerness to please wiggles all through his little body.

We are the same as we trust more and more in our Master and can begin to live and breathe our prayers. As we progress, we reach the point where "we cease not" in praying, but prayer flows through mind and body and comes out in everyday living — the blessed joy of living in the Spirit of the Lord, or "living our prayers."

Many others are taught by the Master himself as they look and listen through the distinct examples He gives each of us.

Always God works through our diverse and unique personalities so we won't become afraid of an unfamiliar custom or practice and stand shut off from others in His creative world forever.

Chapter Four, Symbols of God's Communication

This is my most personal chapter, because in it, I have revealed my inner self, how God has touched me. Despite the risk, it has been extremely exciting to me to reflect and actually put these moments down on paper. Wow!

I know that some of the instances might be hard to accept. But, all of them are true.

We live in such a facade-like world. Most of the time we wear a face that we think will gain us acceptance. If you were to sit next to me or in front of me at a Lady Bears basketball game at Southwest Missouri State University, you might not guess that I am a Christian. My extremely human nature comes out like gangbusters as I watch the opposing Zebras whistle a foul.

And so this book is also for the handsome young couple that often sat in front of George

Epilogue

and me at those Lady Bear games. I know at times I must have infuriated them with my "enthusiasm." I wish now they knew who I *really* am — the sometimes wayward, but ultimately kind and obedient *child of a loving God.*

Just as God has often shown His closeness to me through earthly symbols, I in turn want to follow His example and encourage you to look for God's communication around you.

Chapter Five, Peace — Gathering Strength

Now I see the importance of the places and times of our lives where nothing seems to move — the "plateaus." The balance we acquire at these times is phenomenal.

I came to a better understanding of God through thoughts, words, songs and listening skills. His way of reaching you may be different. *Listen.*

Most importantly during these spiritual plateaus, I learned the value of obedience. An old saint once told me that "faith is not believing in spite of the circumstances, but obedience in spite of the consequences." What a valuable learning tool to realize this lesson was open-ended — that God was forming and molding me to His ultimate will — and stubborn me was enjoying it!

Chapter Six, Trusting in His Promises

I have never been a strong advocate of the color pink, yet God directed this chapter to be colored pink and named: "Trusting in His Promises."

In reading this chapter again, I am amazed to see not only God's constancy in my life, but the total turning over of my responses to Him, trusting and believing and "faithing," as I came to call this child-like trust that came over me.

In this chapter the focus was on God's love, support and guidance to one of His own — and the realization that He was deeply involved in my life. (Remember, I allowed Him to be, praise God.)

I learned so much in this valley. Most of all, I wanted to climb back up and share all I was learning in the vale times. As I write this now, dear reader, I am very much aware that you are a part of that experience (as much as you are disposed to be).

Chapter Seven, Holy Spirit: Cause and Effect

I am usually a very talkative person. But it is when I am quiet that I receive the information that comes from the One on high. Now, George, my husband, is also a great listener and a blessing as well as a balm of oil to my creative mind. His gentle support soothes me. God was so good when He matched the two of us together in such harmony.

God can be thought of as a loving and protective husband, and in my eyes the perfect father. As I have read and re-read what has been written here about the Holy Spirit, I realize how He is the very Breath of God. And how in His faithfulness He has become my breath, too.

In some form or fashion of Himself, the Holy Spirit, is always guiding, directing, and caring for me. It is beyond me how all of this happens, but when a person is so totally involved with God, then comes a broader understanding that we "can do all things through Christ who strengthens" *us*.

You can go beyond your human understanding or abilities. I recall Jesus saying to His disciples, "You will do even greater things than these..." wonders that He had been working. Not that we are better than Christ, but I've learned to listen and to trust and to share the Lord and through that He is able to work His wonders. Amen.

Chapter Eight, Tempered Steel

When God molds and refines, many times it feels good. Sometimes we're not even aware of it. Other times, in the tempering fire, it's painful. But God balances the painful times with the knowledge of His closeness to you, His overpowering love, compassion and tender care.

Looking back over my years, and recognizing God's part in refining me to His purpose, I am often surprised. Whether He is gently molding me, or helping me through the fire of a rough time, the joy of the nearness of Him is the same. And I am blessed.

Chapter Nine, Victory

When you cross the finish line, whether you come in first or last (after all, you ran the full race and accomplished the task that was given you), you deserve the medal that says *Victory*.

I envision God slipping the ribbon over each of our heads and saying "Well done, good and faithful child."

Then we naturally drop to our knees — but with shoulders back and head held high, we can look full into the absorbing love of God, and receive our true reward. Amen and amen.